Out of Silence ...

Out of Silence

A Pianist's Yearbook

Susan Tomes

THE BOYDELL PRESS

© Susan Tomes 2010

First published 2010
The Boydell Press, Woodbridge

ISBN 978–1–84383–557–8

The Boydell Press is an imprint of Boydell & Brewer Ltd
PO Box 9, Woodbridge, Suffolk IP12 3DF, UK
and of Boydell & Brewer Inc.
668 Mt Hope Avenue, Rochester, NY 14620, USA
website: www.boydellandbrewer.com

The publisher has no responsibility for the continued existence or accuracy of URLs for external or third-party internet websites referred to in this book, and does not guarantee that any content on such websites is, or will remain, accurate or appropriate.

A CIP record for this book is available from the British Library

This publication is printed on acid-free paper

Printed in Great Britain by
CPI Antony Rowe, Chippenham and Eastbourne

Contents

A note on names

A few names crop up frequently in the book:
Bob is my husband Robert Philip, a music historian. Maya is
my daughter Maya Feile Tomes. My colleagues in the Florestan
Trio are violinist Anthony Marwood and cellist Richard Lester.
György Sebök was the Hungarian piano professor whose
lessons still provide food for thought.

$$P_{reface}$$

One of the questions that members of the public most often ask writers and composers is, 'Where do you get your ideas from?' They don't so often think to ask this question of performers. People who are not themselves musicians tend to assume that if you're playing classical music, you just play the notes and the music comes out sounding right all by itself.

But 'sounding right' is actually the end-point of a long process of preparation which involves everything from historical knowledge to a very subtle appreciation of how things connect and how this might be conveyed in sound. A musical score only supplies a certain amount of information. Although the notes are specified, an enormous amount of additional information is not given, and perhaps never could or should be. Composers know that there's sometimes an inverse relationship between how many detailed instructions they give and how successful the result will be. The reticence of the printed score usually stimulates an imaginative dialogue between the performer and the music. Good performers throw themselves into the task of sensing what layers of meaning are implied by the notes.

So performing musicians need ideas too. And, like writers and composers, we find them in surprising places, sometimes far away from music. In my own particular case, I've long had the feeling that if I learn to 'listen' attentively to events around me, I'll hear answers – often magically relevant ones – to problems that perplex me in music. When I practise by myself, or rehearse with others, I'm often searching for the way to make connections between parts of a piece of music, between melody and harmony, between inner voices, between foreground and background. I wonder about the character of transitional sections, about how to make the overall structure clear, and about why composers can't help being themselves. Solutions, or at least approaches to the problems, are often supplied by non-musical situations which work by analogy and make the current of understanding flow more easily when I next sit down at the piano. Something overheard on a train or read in a newspaper, the expression on a face, how an animal moves: anything that we experience can teach us how things connect. And the connections between things lie at the heart of what musicians call 'interpretation'.

All the entries in this book, even if they seem just to be about everyday events, are there because they provided some kind of analogy which helped to move me a stage further in whatever my artistic task was at the time. So for example when I write about the way a tennis player returns the ball, or the way a diver enters the water, it's because it showed me something about how musicians behave, how to analyse a process, or how to imagine an element of performance. It's by listening for connections, both in art and life, that I feel I'm entering into the same kind of thought process that my favourite composers did. As Schumann said about himself, 'Everything that happens in the world affects me: literature, people, politics. I mull it all over in my own way, and it finds an outlet in my music.'

January . . .

Six o'clock in the morning

I had to set my alarm for 6 o'clock in the morning to drive to the airport. Whenever I set my alarm for that time, it evokes a particular memory. It's like Bill Murray's alarm clock in the film *Groundhog Day*, clicking round implacably to the fateful moment, waking him with a jolt every morning at the same hour in an unending sequence.

As a schoolchild, I used to get up at 6am every day to practise the piano before I went to school, and 6am is still That Time for me. In Edinburgh it was dark, of course, or it feels now as if it was always dark, as well as freezing cold. My round metal blue alarm clock would jiggle noisily on the chest of drawers, and I would half-fall out of bed in the attempt to bang it on the crown of its head to stop it. Our house was not centrally heated and there was no heating in my bedroom. At first I got washed, dressed and grumpily went straight to the piano, but after a while my piano teacher decreed that I must eat something before I began to practise. This was a welcome innovation because it meant I could delay the start of my practising by slowly eating a bowl of cereal. Eventually, my delaying tactic was rumbled, and I had to set the alarm ten minutes earlier to allow for the cereal. I was grumpy because it struck me as unfair that I had to get up while my parents were still in bed.

I began my practice with scales and arpeggios, which eventually I could do on automatic pilot, thinking about something completely different (often making up stories in my

11

head). My main practice was devoted to the three piano pieces I had to prepare for my lesson. Between pieces, I popped over to the electric bar fire and crouched down to warm my hands. Finally, my favourite bit, when I was allowed to play through something new just for fun. I was a good sight-reader and had an insatiable appetite for what Dave Eggers calls 'non-required reading'. My mother sympathised and was always borrowing music from the library for me, or buying me albums like *Jewels from the Ballet, Favourite Strauss Waltzes, Oklahoma* and *Russ Conway's Piano Magic*. By now Dad would be in the kitchen putting the finishing touches to the family's cooked breakfast of bacon, sausage, beans, black pudding and fried bread, a meal my sisters and I loved on those cold mornings, but an example of the kind of diet which was later implicated in Scotland's obesity crisis.

The idea of getting up early in the morning to practise the piano was not mine. It arose because there was so much homework to do when I got home from school, and the amount increased as the years went by. Especially when I started playing the violin as a second instrument, taking music theory exams, and eventually learning percussion too, there just wasn't enough time to fit everything in. I left the house at 8am to get the bus to school. When I got home, often after 5pm if we had orchestra practice, hockey or debating after school, I was tired. It was scarcely possible to embark then on piano practice, violin practice, and a couple of hours of school homework. So my mother decided there was no alternative but for me to start my day earlier. In due course, my piano teacher said I should really be doing more than the hour and a half I was fitting in before leaving for school. I added a second burst of piano practice in the afternoons, though perhaps burst is the wrong word. Looking back on the teenage years when I did my national school exams, it seems to me that I was on the go from before 6am until bedtime with scarcely a moment to stare out of the window (an activity which I now treasure). In a way, I never had such an intense timetable again, at least not day after day and month after month like that.

I was caught in a pincer movement operated by my mother and my piano teacher. I resisted, even though I did basically like playing the piano. My mother always said that I would thank her in the end (and she was right). But, like so many other youngsters in that position, I felt that I was practising to gratify someone other than myself. My teacher was pleased with me, my mother was pleased with me, and from time to time I got to play in a concert and realised that other people enjoyed hearing me play as well. I got enough positive feedback to justify the effort. Left to my own devices, however, I would never have set that alarm for 6am of my own volition.

In my student years, both at music college and later at university, I had a prolonged crisis about practising. This too seems to be very common amongst musicians who've already notched up years and years of practice by the time they leave school. When it was up to me to decide whether to practise or not, I felt completely at sea. My mother was no longer alive by then. Nobody was going to prod me into getting up; in fact by the time I got to university nobody would have reproached me if I hadn't practised at all. Nevertheless I found it very hard to forge any schedule of my own. I still felt kind of mutinous about practising, even when there was nobody to mutiny against.

It dawned on me eventually that I had to make the transition from reading someone else's script for my life to writing my own. I think I'd always found a certain perverse satisfaction in telling myself I was only practising because someone else had made me. *I* wasn't the insufferable prig who actually wanted to get up while it was still dark to play the piano. I only did it because I was made to, didn't I? But now, if I was going to continue with any kind of purpose, or even become a professional musician, I had to choose it of my own accord – if we ever make 'free' choices. I was the one who had to want to do it, and I wasn't sure if I did. It took years – probably into my thirties – before I was sure I was playing the piano because I wanted to, rather than because someone else wished it. Had I wanted it all along?

$\mathcal{B}$ilbao

The first concert of the year always brings a mixture of feelings. A break from daily piano practice over Christmas and New Year is welcome, partly because time away from the instrument provides an opportunity for that mysterious thing, appetite, to make itself felt again. I often practise simply because I *have* to, so it's good to be reminded of what it feels like to play because I *want* to.

My first concert of this year is with my trio, the Florestan Trio, at the Philharmonic Society in Bilbao, one of Spain's oldest concert societies. When I first played there, I rather hoped the Spanish audience would be hugely demonstrative, standing on their seats and cheering. In fact, the Bilbao audience is very reserved and dignified, a characteristic I've come to like now that I've understood a bit more about the seriousness of this northern city, with people hurrying about in their berets and winter coats in the rain. I like to take a newspaper into a café and watch them dispatch their morning espressos *con brio* on their way to work, every inch the proud architects of modern Spain.

The Philharmonic Society Hall in Bilbao is like a Spanish counterpart of the Wigmore Hall in London, with its cosy old 'green room' full of photographs of artists who've played there during the last hundred years. It's always touching to be surrounded by visual evidence of musicians from earlier decades,

14

and it comes as rather a shock to think that we ourselves are part of that line. So many of those earlier performers, particularly the Spanish ones, have a fiery dark glamour which makes me literally pale in comparison.

Coming off stage, I realise I have been holding my breath, as I often do in concerts. Sometimes I only realise it when I've done so for long enough to provoke a fit of explosive coughing, difficult to combine with graceful piano playing. It's very contrary of me to hold my breath, because when I'm on stage I have the feeling that playing to a large audience is the equivalent of *exhaling* hugely. It helps to imagine myself radiating out to the listeners, especially because, as a pianist, I don't actually face them and therefore don't have a natural chance to establish a rapport. Before I start to play, I sometimes try to summon up a mental image of myself at the piano like the sun in the centre of a child's drawing, its rays fanning out into the hall. Occasionally the audience seems to send back its own reciprocal rays of warmth.

Against this background thought of 'breathing out' over the audience, it's perplexing to find myself holding my breath. The effort of communicating with the listeners, projecting sound to the back of the darkened hall, seems to be counteracted by a need to conserve my own forces. I want to give, but need to find a way to do it without feeling depleted. This is a constant battle which seems to open new fronts all the time. Some musicians speak of drawing energy from the music, others of drawing strength from the audience. Certainly one needs to find a balance between breathing out and breathing in, or one wouldn't last long as a performer. I remind myself of the literal meaning of 'inspiration'.

Music for the right time of day

Enforced waiting time in the airport has become the trio's opportunity to hold admin meetings. On the journey home from Bilbao, we use the time to discuss programmes for some upcoming concerts, trying to tailor our choice of music to the time of day at which the concert takes place. Most of the concerts are in the evening, but some are 'coffee concerts' on a Sunday morning, others are lunchtime events, and one is a late-night programme.

In Western music we haven't been particularly sensitive to what time of day our music is performed. Classical musicians often grumble amongst themselves about how difficult it is to get geared up for a performance of something heavy and emotional, like late Romantic music, in the morning. For a coffee concert, we try to find something fresh and lively. For a late-night concert, we try to find something sultry, quirky or contemplative – something a little bit off the beaten track. But in general, our repertoire seems to sit most happily in the mid-evening slot, the most popular time for concerts, when people have finished their work for the day and are ready for a couple of hours of meat-and-potatoes listening.

When I was on tour in India as a young professional, I had an encounter I've never forgotten. We had been asked at short notice to share a concert with a group of Indian classical musicians, but it was not yet certain at what time of day the event would be. Our Indian colleagues asked us what our programme would be if the concert were in the morning. 'Haydn and Brahms', we said. And what would it be if the concert were in the evening? 'Haydn and Brahms', we said. They looked baffled. 'But that is the same as you said for the morning!' 'Yes', we said, 'we'd present the same programme in either case'. We asked them what they would play. 'If the concert is in the morning, we will improvise on a morning raga, and if it is in the evening we will play one of the evening ragas – depending on the hour', they said.

They were telling us that in the Indian classical tradition each time of day has its musical counterpart. So the time of the performance would determine which raga was used by the players for improvising; it would be nonsensical to play evening music in the morning, or the other way round. As I took in this concept, it seemed very clear to me that they were right and we were wrong. How could we glibly have said, 'Haydn and Brahms', whenever the concert was?

We tried to explain that Western listeners are quite happy for music to impose its own atmosphere on the time of day. But even in our ears this did not quite ring true. Indeed, we had often complained how hard it was to concentrate on rehearsing Brahms (weighty, sensuous, emotional) at breakfast-time, or how jarring it could feel to play Haydn (clever, spirited, transparent) in the late evening. In this respect we were unknowingly in tune with the Indian view that music should reflect the rise and fall of the day, the change of light and air.

When our shared Anglo-Indian concert eventually landed at 4pm, and we found ourselves sweating over the Brahms C major Trio in a sundrenched garden in Pune, teacups clinking in the background, we felt a new respect for our Indian friends' understanding of the delicate harness between music and the hours of the day.

*P*latform *N*erves

Going on stage at the Wigmore Hall for today's lunchtime concert, which is being broadcast live on radio, I tried out a method of calming nerves that was described to me by a student – to listen with full attention to the sound of the audience's clapping, hearing it as a positive thing in itself, a sound event with its own character and its own shape, rising and falling. It does help to throw one's attention away from oneself during that strange little journey between the stage door and the piano stool, often done to the soundtrack of one's heart thumping.

My friend Greg, trained as a classical ballet dancer, told me that dancers combat nerves by planning exactly how that little journey from the wings will be accomplished. How many steps, with what tempo, to what point of arrival, and what graceful gesture to make when they get there. He was very amused when I said that no music teacher had ever discussed bowing with me, let alone such niceties as whether to drop one's head forward and whether to maintain eye contact with the audience while bowing, or how to turn from the audience and sit down on the piano stool (which as he rightly pointed out can be an ungraceful moment). After all these years of giving concerts I admit that my platform behaviour remains a bit hit-and-miss, and the same goes for most of my colleagues. It has somehow never seemed appropriate to consider the choreography of getting to the piano, and I am not convinced the audience considers it all that important either. Musicians who are 'too good' at it almost inspire disbelief.

When the topic of platform nerves came up recently with a group of students, someone mentioned a well-known piece of advice: visualise the audience sitting there in their underwear. Apparently this helps to divest the audience of its threatening look, though I don't think the image would be a helpful one for me, because it would make them seem comical instead, and that's not how I want to see them. My Swedish clarinettist friend Kjell Fagéus has a wonderful image which he has used to the great benefit of students. It derives from the behaviour of his neighbour's child, William, a four-year-old boy at the time. William was a confident boy and loved to wander next door and visit Kjell and his wife. Without knocking, William would simply fling the front door open and shout, 'Here I am! Do you want to play with me?' His sense of being welcome was so great that the adults always stopped what they were doing and went to join in a game. It didn't seem possible to disappoint him. Some time later it occurred to Kjell how marvellous it would be if one could learn something from William's attitude when going on stage as a performer. He told the story to his students, some of whom say they still think of it when waiting to go on to the platform. They find that walking towards the audience with the conscious thought, 'Here I am! Do you want me to play?' gives them a new feeling of light-hearted security.

Keys from the Ice Age

A piano tuner in Brussels, discussing the scarcity of ivory for piano keys, tells me that a new source of ivory is coming onto the market. Because of climate change, the permafrost is beginning to melt in certain remote regions of Russia, exposing the long-frozen bodies of woolly mammoths from the Ice Age. Their ivory tusks are still well enough preserved to be used for carving. As mammoths are already extinct, they cannot be an endangered species, and at the moment it is legal to use mammoth ivory, which is in fact enjoying a bit of a renaissance amongst craftsmen in Siberia and Alaska.

I'm astonished to think of slivers of deep-frozen tusk from thousands of years ago finding their way onto piano keyboards for the performance of Chopin and Liszt, and incidentally giving a fresh slant to that hackneyed phrase, 'a mammoth programme'. Mammoth ivory on a Steinway reminds me of Russell Hoban's musings in his *Turtle Diary*. Visiting the aquarium, one of the characters reads a sign noting that turtles are the source of turtle soup and also of tortoiseshell spectacle frames, and wonders why turtles should be the source of precisely those unpredictable things, rather than others. 'Why soup, why spectacles?' he asks.

$\mathcal{K}$ilmainham $\mathcal{J}$ail

I wake in Dublin to leaden skies and gusts of rain, weather which seems to frown and remind me I'm not on holiday. On a concert day, even if I'm technically free until the evening (which is only the case if I'm already in the right city and have already done the rehearsals) I know from experience that I shouldn't tire myself out by trailing about the city as a tourist. It's a bad feeling to reach the evening and realise that I'm mentally or physically tired before I've even played a note. Typically, concerts now begin at 8pm (it used to be 7.30pm, but 8pm is gradually becoming more common) and I'm still playing at 10pm. On a non-concert day I'd be starting to wind down for bed at this time, but on a concert day I must not only be wide awake, but at my liveliest. So on the day of my Dublin concert I don't want to travel into the city centre and spend hours walking around before going to the hall to do some private practice.

On the other hand, my hotel is right opposite a historic building which all the guidebooks recommend. This is Kilmainham Jail, where many Irish 'rebels' – that's to say, against the British rulers – were imprisoned at various periods between the eighteenth and twentieth centuries. Our guide is a fount of information and is clearly used to savouring its effect on her flock, many of whom are American. She tells us about the suffering of Irish prisoners at the hands of the

British, especially after the uprising in 1916 when all the ring-leaders were executed here in the jail. The tour finishes in the yard where this happened. It's still raining, and the grey stone matches the sky. All of us on the tour are moved and silent, particularly after she tells us of the fate of one of the ringleaders who was injured in the uprising and too weak to walk unaided to his execution. They brought him in on a stretcher ...

The impact of this visit to the jail lasts all day (and beyond). It undoubtedly alters my mood during my performance of Mozart's G Major Concerto in the National Concert Hall that evening. Somehow the gentle and lovely music now feels like my private attempt to atone for these wrongs, or at least to provide some consolation – though I realise this is purely a fantasy, and that nobody else knows my thoughts. Could it be, I wonder, that anyone listening would intuit a solemn quality in my playing that evening, or is it thoroughly hidden? For myself, I'll remember that performance as the postlude to standing in the rain in Stonebreakers' Yard – which, as the guide told us, was chosen for the last act in that story because it was not overlooked either from within or from without.

Learning a Craft

In Dublin, on the morning after playing my Mozart concerto, I visit the beautiful Chester Beatty Library and its exhibition of texts from different faiths.

Reading that Zen appealed to the warrior class in Japan because it didn't stress the study of texts or the elaborate observation of ritual, but rather the cultivation of a bright mind through action and long self-discipline, I'm reminded of Richard Sennett's recent book, *The Craftsman.* He writes of the long training which enables a craftsman patiently to master his materials and, through the exercise of great discipline, to attain a focus and a result not available to those who don't undergo long training or the pursuit of excellence.

This has many parallels with the practice of music. And maybe this is what should be known and valued about the study of a musical instrument. Leaving aside for a moment the vexed question of whether serious music has appeal for today's world, there is still – behind the music – the great hinterland of craft, apprenticeship, and the humble acquiring of a skill which enables a person to learn not just the skill but also the means of understanding themselves, or at least of witnessing themselves in a challenging and revealing activity. Perhaps not enough attention is given to the benefits of a years-long training like this. We're now so used to encountering people who seem to start their jobs with minimal training and minimal knowledge, but maximum confidence and self-satisfaction. 'Selling' has become the principal focus of activity, and it seems that you can do it from your first day in the job. We hardly know how to appraise someone whose training has been going on for years, who devotes hours of every day to keeping up a high level of familiarity with a complex task. Such a person undoubtedly develops levels of concentration which are out of the ordinary, and it could well be viewed as a kind of spiritual training, not aimed at a religious goal but at the same kind of 'awakeness' which Japanese warriors – and other Zen students – aspired to.

The goal beyond music: is this sufficiently emphasised? Training and practice are forms of self-development highly valued in some cultures. Learning to play a musical instrument should be seen as a valuable process in its own right, even if the purely musical result is unreliable. When families suffer through the early stages of a youngster learning the violin, for example, they should remember that the scratchy melodies are not the only product of the enterprise. Everybody 'gets it' when they watch high-level sporting events and competitions. They see that the training, the endurance and the self-denial for a greater goal are all worthy pursuits which bring benefits quite apart from the medals and prize money. But then, of course, everyone has a body. We can all imagine using it more fully, so it's easier to imagine dedicating ourselves to a sporting goal.

When I think about my own state of mind on the day of a well-prepared performance, I realise that it's sharpened to a remarkable extent. It's as if everything is slowed down so that I am aware of every little detail, and the gaps in between the little details. Things that happen around me seem to happen rather slowly and loosely. I get irritable with people who don't seem to be on the same mental fast track. At the same time, I realise that my sharpened concentration is directed primarily to one end, the piece I'm going to perform. It's as if a beam of light is directed from my head towards this one thing. There's a link between brain and hand: hand which runs continually through the physical sequence of movements

– though not always in a predictable order – needed to play the piece. Is the hand in the mind, or the mind in the hand? So closely do they collaborate that it sometimes feels like one, sometimes the other. Certainly it feels as if the hand 'knows'.

There's a difference between a skill which is grounded in physical practice, and other forms of work where mental grasp alone is sufficient. I think this is something that non-musicians don't always understand – that quite apart from the mental skill required, there has to be the physical skill needed to make the instrument do what you want. The spirit has to be willing, but the flesh has to be willing too! Indeed the physical skill is paramount in actually being able to produce music that means something to the listener. I can think of many clever people who sit in their offices and at their desks producing excellent work, yet without ever having to master a mediating instrument, the means by which their skill is relayed to the world. Some musicians – composers, conductors – don't have an instrument (or singing voice) to contend with. As a result, executant musicians often feel that composers and conductors are in a different category of musician. Understanding music and being able to make it sound are skills not always found in the same person, and sometimes the task of actually playing music is underestimated by those who don't do it.

A more precise profession

A friend of mine has got fed up with trying to make a living as a singer, and has re-trained and gone into the banking profession. He told me that shortly after joining his new bank, one of his colleagues said to him, 'It must be strange, going from a very imprecise profession to a very precise one.' To his great credit my ex-singer friend replied, 'Actually, it's the other way round. Music is a lot more precise than banking.' I love the surprising inversion of this remark, all the more because it just popped out spontaneously.

'It's true, though', said my friend later when we were laughing about it. 'In banking, a lot of my work isn't directly to do with figures. Of course you have to be extremely accurate now and then, when it's required. In music, you have to be accurate *all the time*.'

O_n adding music

A classical music item pops up today on my internet news page with the review of a piano recital by young students in Jamaica. Evidently the young pianists played their prescribed pieces somewhat stiffly and mechanically, and the reviewer commented that this was 'only to be expected with classical music'. This reminds me of Alice Munro's alarming description of a concert given by children, at the end of one of her short stories, where she describes the startling appearance of a talented player in amongst the plodders at a recital given by students of a local piano teacher. The listening parents are amazed by the sounds flowing from the talented one's fingers. 'The last thing anyone had expected was *music*', says Munro tartly.

A friend recently came back from a teaching trip to Korea. He reported that his piano students would dutifully turn up and play their pieces with great accuracy but no feeling, like clever robots. Eventually he figured out that this was their way of showing great respect for the score, and for the revered teacher, whose views on interpretation had not yet been vouchsafed to them. They practised carefully and mechanically, for technical security, waiting for their teacher to pronounce on their readiness for the next level. He realised that he had to 'give them permission to add music', as he put it. Once told that they could now play musically, his students suddenly relaxed and played with feeling and relish, as if they had just been waiting for this moment. He commented that it was the exact reverse of the situation he was used to encountering in Britain, where students plunge in with feeling and relish, but never get around to establishing technical security. He was so used to exhorting his pupils to be more attentive to detail, and to make everything more accurate and reliable, that he was quite thrown by the experience of his Korean students who had done so as a first step, and were humbly holding back from adding music. When released from their self-imposed restraint, they went flying ahead like arrows loosed from powerful bows.

Not everyone can thrive, however, on a security-first, music-later strategy. Perhaps it's as much a matter of temperament as of cultural outlook. György Sebők said that if you insist on practising mechanical finger exercises, you should make sure to choose pieces which were designed purely as exercises. He thought that if you practised the difficult passages in your Mozart piano concerto mechanically, it would destroy your rapport with the music. In my own experience, a blend of approaches is what works best. I still feel that looking for the right musical character and mood should always be the very first step, never a process which is deliberately delayed. All too often you hear students and even professionals playing routinely because they are 'still getting to know the notes'. To me, this is nonsense. Getting to know the notes is an unbearably tedious process unless the appetite for the musical result precedes it. You have to learn how to be creatively impatient with yourself during the note-learning stage. If you've already imagined how you want the music to sound, the learning process will flow much faster, and along the right grooves. You have to look for the musical impulse right away, or it's like trying to drive a car with no fuel in the tank.

Chopin loses to 'Danny Boy'

When I was little, and learning to play the piano, my mother sometimes asked me to play to our relatives when they came to visit us in Edinburgh. Their tastes were more towards light music, but they enjoyed seeing their little niece playing a grand piano.

When I was about eleven or twelve, one of my aunts submitted to a short performance. I had just finished learning a fast and intricate Chopin Fantasie-Impromptu, probably the hardest thing I'd learned so far. I felt nervous playing it to my aunt who sat behind me on the flowery sofa in the attitude of secret resistance she always assumed for classical music. I came to the end of the piece and turned around. Passing over without comment what had just occurred, she asked, 'Could you play "Danny Boy"?' 'Danny Boy' is a lovely Irish melody that I knew by ear. I hadn't ever thought to play it on the piano, but I played it then for my aunt, filling in what seemed like suitable harmonies with my left hand. It lasted about a minute. I turned round to see her sitting there with tears pouring down her cheeks. Danny Boy had scored where Chopin had failed to touch her.

This experience has stayed with me, and in a way I never quite got over the brutal contrast between my aunt's rejection of Chopin and her dissolving submission to an old folksong melody which clearly said 'music' to her where Chopin said only 'cleverness'.

Confidences from a stranger

A letter arrives from a retired professor who has been writing to me now and then since reading *Beyond the Notes*. We have never met, but having read my book he feels he can write to me frankly about music and the role it plays in his recovery from a long illness. Today he writes that he has been very ill again since his last big operation. He describes a few days in a hospice. Waking early in the morning and unable to get back to sleep, he puts on a CD from a box set of late Beethoven string quartets, intending to listen to his favourite, the quartet Opus 127. By mistake, though, he puts on the Opus 130 quartet which ends with the enormous fugue, the *Grosse Fuge*. This titanic struggle with intractable material he describes as having an overwhelming impact on him, as a powerful performance of *King Lear* once did in the theatre. Tears poured down his face, he writes, as he listened to the musicians grappling with Beethoven's unlikeable fugue. He writes of the terror which this and other works inspire, now that he is in a frightening phase of his own life.

I have never met this man, and I feel simultaneously upset on his behalf, amazed that he would write about such things to a virtual stranger, and awestruck by the power of music to penetrate people so deeply – particularly as Beethoven's *Great Fugue* has always passed me by on another wavelength, its heavings and groanings in a language I don't truly understand.

Since my early days as a professional musician I have been surprised by the way that performing music confers temporarily on me (and other musicians) the powers of a shaman. Listeners evidently feel that because they have heard and seen us communicate with music written centuries ago and brought to life in their presence, we must be capable of some kind of mediation between things seen and unseen. Over the years many people have confided in me, after concerts, things which they would not dream of divulging if they only met me at dinner. I realise that I am borrowing some kind of power from the music, but it feels good; I relish the sudden opening-up of new channels of communication. People now sometimes respond to my books about music in the same way. After living with a book on their bedside table for days or weeks, they come to feel that the author is a friend, and it feels natural to confide in that friend. For me this is actually one of the most precious things about being a musician, and one of the things I would most miss if I stopped.

February ...

A row of sforzandi

Doing some practice on Beethoven's C minor piano trio for an upcoming performance, I remember my coaching sessions at the Banff School of the Arts in Canada with the Hungarian violinist Zoltán Székely, who moved there in his later years. Székely had been a friend and recital partner of the composer Béla Bartók, and he founded the Hungarian String Quartet. He was revered in Banff as a deeply serious musician representative of the middle-European musical heritage.

We were discussing with him this very Beethoven trio. Beethoven had written a passage marked 'piano'. During this passage, there were several 'sf' markings, indicating sudden little accents. There was a row of these sforzandi, a bar or two apart. At the end of the quiet passage, Beethoven had written 'forte', but there was no crescendo written between the 'piano' and the 'forte', just this row of sforzandi.

The question was, whether by writing a row of sudden accents, Beethoven was implying a crescendo, or whether it was correct to play the whole passage quietly with the accents just popping out without disturbing the basic dynamic. In other words, we were debating whether to create a gradual incline from the quiet to the loud, or whether to create a terrace, suddenly stepping from the lower level to the higher at the moment when Beethoven had marked 'loud'. This had been the subject of minor discussion in our private rehearsal, but not much, because to be honest the music seemed to work either way and we didn't mind leaving it open to the whim of the moment.

However, Székely did not look at it in this light. He was inclined to the view that a row of sforzando markings meant a crescendo, on the grounds that you do not keep insisting on something (the sforzando markings being the insisting) without getting louder and more heated. Therefore it would be natural to get louder with each one. But Beethoven had not actually said 'get louder', and of course he was quite capable of doing so, as he had done elsewhere in the movement. Székely suspected he knew what Beethoven wanted, but he was in an agony of mind in case he was about to supplant Beethoven's vision with his own lesser brand.

He paced the room, staring out of the window, muttering to himself, 'Which is right? It could be done that way. But is it right? Should we allow ourselves to get louder, or not?' He seemed troubled, lost in thought. 'Let us try it both ways.' We tried it both ways, but that didn't clarify matters. 'It is convincing like that, yes. But is it right? That is the question. Do we have the right to get louder, or must we resist, for Beethoven's sake?' He paced back and forth looking anguished. Lunchtime came and went as we proceeded in tiny little increments towards a decision, which under his guidance we took with the utmost humility, knowing that we must leave room for revision if a higher truth was revealed. It was simultaneously admirable and repellent.

Afterwards, our American cellist said it was that lesson which made him feel he didn't want to be a classical musician after all. He imagined a future of beating his breast over tiny decisions which were probably beside the point for the majority of musicians as well as listeners, yet which seemed of immutable importance for middle-European devotees. Székeley's was a very un-British, obsessive commitment to the 'truth' of the composer's markings. It was like an old Jewish scholar poring again and again over the words of the Torah, scrutinising them for meaning.

$\mathcal{T}_{oo\ good?}$

The trio is in Vienna to perform in the beautiful Konzerthaus, one of my favourite halls in Europe. At the end of the evening, there's a drinks reception, and one of the guests comes to say that he had enjoyed our performance. 'I couldn't help wondering, though,' he says, 'if it was just too good?' I ask what he meant by 'too good'. He replies, 'Everything tonight seemed so well-played and well thought-out, all the notes exactly right. Was that what Beethoven expected? I imagine that in his day everything would have been rougher, lots of wrong notes, more hit and miss. Wouldn't they have thrown the performance together at the last minute? I couldn't help wondering what Beethoven would have made of your polished performance.'

This is a tricky area when one speaks about 'authentic' performance of music from earlier centuries. It's probably true that Beethoven and his friends would have approached it all differently. For a start, they would have been playing these works in someone's living-room or drawing-room, not to a silent respectful audience in a large concert hall. They probably would have had very little rehearsal; their groups might have used a mixture of amateurs and professionals, and no doubt there was a great variety of technical standards in their playing. Of course there were professional musicians in Beethoven's day, and there were virtuosi too – including

Beethoven himself. But I think it's been amply proved that musicians were not in the habit of practising for such long hours or as systematically as they do today. No doubt their playing was often inspired, but the prevailing standard was probably not as reliable as it is now.

We have been trained by recordings to expect note-perfect performances. Our hi-fi systems and our digital surround-sound televisions have made it possible to scrutinise the pixels of music. Even when musicians try to obtain instruments like the ones that Beethoven would have had at his disposal, there's a limit to how far they want to copy the conditions prevailing in Beethoven's time. Trying to evoke the precise sound quality of an early instrument is one thing, but hit-and-miss performance is another. How far could one go in trying to be faithful to the conditions of the original run-through? Breaking strings, out of tune playing, squeaking and scratching, missing notes, players stopping if they got lost – all perfectly natural when amateurs get together in the privacy of someone's home, but not transferable to the paying audience of today. I always imagine that if we could travel back in time and attend one of Beethoven's soirées, we might be amazed by the standard of playing they tolerated and found perfectly convincing.

We always try to approach as near as we can to what we in our twenty-first-century mindset consider the ideal performance, using all the advantages of modern instruments and the stability that they possess. Beethoven to us is not a messy, lumbering giant but an almost godlike creator whose every word is worth weighing. We acknowledge the delib-erate roughness in his music, but we still want to play it with polish. But in trying to be so polished, perhaps we overshoot the mark. We have been so influenced by the magnifying lens of the silent concert hall. Is playing as well as possible the same as doing justice to the music?

A plate of salad in the corner

Last night I went to a house concert at which a violinist and pianist gave a duo recital in someone's living-room, a try-out concert for a performance later in the week in a concert hall. We sat just yards away from them during the whole two-hour programme.

When the recital was over, the audience moved their chairs away to create space for tables of food and drink. People moved about, chatting. The two musicians, who had been recovering in an adjacent room, now re-joined us, still wearing their concert outfits. As they entered the room, their cheeks still flushed from the excitement of performing, they looked into the eyes of the people nearest them, who turned away, pretending they hadn't noticed or didn't recognise the musicians. There was, of course, no chance that they hadn't recognised them; we'd all been gazing at them for two solid hours, and at close quarters under the same lights, so there was no way that the listeners could say 'you looked different off the stage', as people often do after public concerts.

As the two players moved unhindered through the little throng, I was fascinated by the way people ignored them. Was it shyness, embarrassment, fear of not knowing what to say? Did they feel awkward about seeing the 'priestly' artist come among them?

I sometimes feel there's a surge of relief among the listeners when the concert is over. It's as if they suddenly think, 'We've been sitting quietly for your benefit for a long time. Now this is our time. We want to drink and talk, put the music behind us. This is part of the evening we've equally looked forward to. We'd like the musicians just to disappear tactfully now.' It's as if the players sink down, the audience rises up, the waves close over the musicians' heads, and the audience takes centre-stage with joyful momentum. They quite resent having to be dragged back to what they thought of the musical evening.

For this same reason, the celebratory suppers at the end of music festivals and so on are often a bit of an anti-climax for me. On such occasions it can sometimes feel as if the music and the musicians were only a catalyst for all the helpers and organisers to bond and have a reason to let their hair down, while the exhausted performers sit quietly in the corner with a plate of salad, everyone carefully avoiding them.

Mendelssohn and Schumann

While learning Mendelssohn's *Variations Sérieuses*, it has some-times flashed through my mind that there are distinct similari-ties between some of his variations and the opening movement of Schumann's first Piano Trio in D minor, a favourite piece of mine and of the Florestan's. The Schumann trio was written after the Mendelssohn. The two composers were friends and Schumann was a warm admirer of Mendelssohn's own D minor piano trio, in the same key as the *Variations Sérieuses*. It's perfectly possible that he was also influenced by Mendelssohn's finest piano piece.

I could show on paper that the Mendelssohn *Variations* and Schumann's Trio have things in common and nobody would contradict me, but this doesn't seem to be enough for me. I somehow have to prove it to myself subjectively as well as objectively, but the subjective proof is much harder to come by and seems to involve a kind of subconscious weighing process. After I've had the initial thought that Schumann may have been inspired by this specific Mendelssohn piece, it starts to bubble in my musical imagination in a strange way. I find myself obsessively going over the phrases, particles of phrases, and in particular the intervals between notes, first as they occur in the Mendelssohn, and then as they happen in Schumann. I sing them under my breath, comparing to see whether they are only similar on the surface, or deeper down as well. I weigh the little musical units in my mind, balancing them against one another for comparative densities.

For a period of weeks, I do this over and over, testing my theory that the two works are related. And I don't just mean that I check my theory intellectually. What I'm searching for is some kind of poetical 'click', or some kind of mental 'ping' such as you get when you strike a wine glass with a fork. Whatever musical truth underlies the Mendelssohn piece – the impulse behind the expression of exactly those notes – has to underlie the similar phrases of the Schumann piece. I test and re-test them in my inner ear as though there is some kind of trial awaiting my expert judgement. Until the trial reaches a conclusion, I am condemned to keep thinking about it. Do all musicians do this kind of obsessive imaginary testing and checking? If it is like this for a mere player, it must be far, far worse for composers!

$\mathcal{E}$xpression marks in letters

A letter arrives from a relative with various remarks whose 'tone' we disagree about. Are they meant seriously, or should we take them humorously? Are they insulting, or said with a twinkle in the eye? Some of us think one thing, some the other; we are all expert at reading between the lines, except that we read different things. It feels important to judge the tone rightly, because we will have to respond. Once again I think about how useful it would be if letters used a system of expressive signals as pieces of music do. Sometimes people in e-mails now use 'emoticons', little symbols with smiley, cross or sad faces to give a clue to whether the writer is serious or joking. But these only graze the surface. I wish there were a system of indicating shades of soft, loud, light, dark, slow and quick, merry and grave, ironical and sorrowful. It happens really quite often that I puzzle over the tone of a written communication, wondering how to 'read' it over and beyond the words at their face value. Indeed, I have often read a whole book under the impression that it was cast in one 'mood', only to discover that the reviewers thought it was clearly in another. You'd think that a skilled writer would know how to embed the appropriate emotions in the choice of words, but however skilful the words are, they often leave matters of 'tone' ambiguous. It's like looking at a musical score with no written instructions about speed, mood, or dynamics. Such scores are common in earlier music, but for some hundreds of years now it's been customary to give at least some indication of tempo and mood. Curiously, this has never developed as an adjunct of literary texts as far as I know, except in stage directions.

Some years ago I read and was blown away by Annie Proulx's novel *The Shipping News*, which I still keep on the shelf next to my desk along with other important books. I read the whole thing under the spell of what I thought was its poignant, regretful tone. Then I discovered that the *Guardian* reviewer had called it 'so funny'. I wrote Annie Proulx a fan letter in which I mentioned that I had been puzzled by the use of the word 'funny' in the review printed on the back cover. She replied, in a little handwritten card which I now keep tucked into the book. She wrote, 'Yes, *Shipping News* is a kind of human comedy. If you missed that element it is because other aspects of the story mattered more to you.' This makes me realise that even had she used little symbols to indicate her tone, I would have missed my own particular truth about her book, and it was one that I wouldn't have missed for anything.

$\mathcal{I}$*nner voices*

After many years of being an amateur wind player, my brother-in-law has given up the French horn and has taken up the viola instead. He feels that playing the horn is getting too strenuous for his lips. I asked him whether he didn't feel this was his opportunity to grab the limelight and take up the violin instead, to have the experience of playing the top line? Or the double bass, to see what it's like at the bottom? He says that having played the French horn for years in wind quintets and orchestras, he finds he has become attached to the role of being a middle voice, and wants to continue in this persona, so he is naturally drawn to the viola. Just as he sees the horn as the mediator of the brass section, he sees the viola as the voice of reason in the strings, rarely getting to sing a glamorous aria, but playing a very important stabilising role. He identifies with this role. We agree that an interest in inner voices is one which marks out a certain kind of musician. There's often so much focus on the leading voice, the top line, the melody instrument, the solo part, and so on, but just as much if not more meaning emanates from the middle voices, often not sufficiently heard or understood. Thank goodness there are people who feel genuinely drawn to playing those middle parts, who see themselves as the binding agent, like eggs in a cake mixture.

There's something in common with the chamber musician

here, though a love of inner voices doesn't quite sum up the chamber musician's passion. For us, it's a little more complicated than that. Chamber players love the diversity of roles they have to play, sometimes being the leader, sometimes a companion, sometimes a supporter or a commentator. They love to find out when they are meant to surge forward, when to step into the limelight, when to comment from the wings, when to contradict, and when to offer another, perhaps more persuasive point of view. They understand that it is a process of layering, and that they must be prepared to explore all the layers. I don't know whether such people are drawn to chamber music because they are open-minded and naturally good listeners, or whether they acquire a tolerant approach along the way, but one thing's for sure: you won't get much out of chamber music unless you genuinely have a live-and-let-live attitude. If you're convinced your own part is the most important all the time, you'd be better off sticking to solo concertos. In chamber music, even the naturally more dominant instruments, such as the piano (or should I say, even the naturally more dominant instrumentalists, like pianists) still have to weave their way in and out of the plot. Chamber music at its best is a vision of the ideal society, where people converse, exchange and are sensitive to one another, respecting one another's territories. It seems to me good preparation for life in a free society.

Driving in the wrong direction

Last night I had another dream about failing to arrive at a Wigmore Hall concert.

I am in a taxi which mysteriously takes a very circuitous route to the Hall. I gradually realise that we are heading out of London and towards Cambridge on the motorway. The driver ignores my pleas to turn around. I try to let my colleagues know that I am stuck, but suddenly my phone will not work. The driver now starts to drive into villages along the way, and stops the taxi here and there, disappearing into houses to talk with the inhabitants. Mysteriously, I am unable to get out of the taxi but am compelled to wait for him to return. He re-appears, I urgently request him to drive as fast as possible to the Wigmore Hall, and we drive on, only to stop somewhere else in the countryside. At one point, I follow him into a building and discover that he is peacefully sitting at a desk, booking his holiday with the help of a travel agent. I plead with him to come out and drive me to my concert.

As we move inexorably away from London, it occurs to me that I could at least try to change into my concert clothes, so that I will be ready to run straight on stage when we arrive at the Wigmore Hall. We stop somewhere new, and I see that there is a theatre nearby. I leave the taxi, run to the backstage door and persuade the staff to let me in so that I can get changed there. They give me the code for the internal door and I wander down a dark maze of corridors with no doors leading to any rooms in which I might take refuge. At the far end of the corridor is a theatre space and I can hear that a performance is in progress. I peep in and see with surprise that all the audience are dressed as bears.

There is nowhere to change, and I return in distress to the taxi. My phone is still not working. I look at my watch and realise that it is 7.40pm, ten minutes after my concert was supposed to begin in central London. It's dark now, nobody knows where I am, and my driver continues imperturbably to head away from where I want to go.

Innocently demanding something difficult

We're starting to plan our masterclasses, in which several student piano trios will come and study with the trio in London over an intensive weekend. We've been talking about the best way to open up the subject for our participants.

Years ago I played the piano for a cello masterclass at the International Musicians' Seminars at Prussia Cove in Cornwall, a wonderful series of courses started by violinist Sándor Végh. In the cello class that year was a rogue member, a horn player who'd begged permission to attend after hearing a coaching session given by the cello professor Johannes Goritzki. There was some sense in it, because the French horn's register does overlap with the cello's, and for that reason, horn players have appropriated certain cello pieces into their own repertoire, as well as sharing some pieces such as the Schumann Adagio and Allegro for horn (or cello) and piano, which my horn-playing friend wanted to play in his lesson.

I played the piano for that lesson with the cello teacher who, not knowing all that much about horn playing, approached the task just as he would have done with a cellist, insisting on the long phrases that Schumann draws over whole bars in slow tempo, demanding increases in dynamic power and expressivity at all climactic points, never letting the horn player get away with a 'neutral' tone when there was a more exact and fitting one to be imagined. Afterwards, the horn player said to

49

me that no horn teacher would have asked for those things, precisely because they are known to be so difficult on the horn. 'Maybe you should have told him they were difficult', I said. 'No, that's just why I like it', said the horn player. 'He has no idea what's hard or not hard on the horn, so he just goes for the best result musically, and he pushes me into areas that no horn teacher would expect me to get into. If I told him that what he was asking was practically impossible, then he'd stop suggesting those things to me, out of sympathy. I don't want that to happen.'

This remark opened up for me the possibility of cross-referencing in advanced teaching. It seemed such a good idea to go for advice to someone in an overlapping field, but someone who doesn't know whether or not it will be hard for you to follow their advice. Often when I'm teaching, I find myself automatically filtering thoughts which I withhold from my student because I don't think they're capable of achieving what I have in mind. Sometimes I press ahead, ask, and get a surprising result which makes us all happy. Other times, though, I insist, make the student anxious and end up by making them stumble in front of their friends. If I fear this kind of result, I try not to press for something out of arm's reach, and instead try to build up in little steps, each of which is achievable.

And of course one mustn't forget that masterclasses are often valuable because a good teacher knows how to demand something they know you can give – or at least suspect that you can. But I think there's a different vein of educational possibility which lies in innocently demanding something you didn't know was difficult.

Always

Rehearsing Debussy's Cello Sonata with cellist Christoph Marks, my colleague in the Gaudier Ensemble, I come upon that printed expression mark in Italian in the last movement which is so sweet and mysterious. It simply says, 'Sempre' – always.

Debussy has some lovely expression marks in his music. A favourite of mine, in the Preludes for piano, is 'En animant surtout dans l'expression', meaning 'becoming more lively, particularly in the expression'. How often is that element neglected by players who think that 'en animant' simply means getting faster! I love the idea that the listener should feel an augmentation in expression before they realise that the music is also picking up speed. Debussy has cleverly identified two elements of 'getting livelier' which can function in tandem, but can also interlock.

I think the single word 'Sempre' in the cello sonata's finale may just be an editor's mistake, or perhaps Debussy's own mistake. Very likely the word 'always' is meant to be attached to the previous instruction. Or perhaps Debussy meant to add on another suggestion like 'always getting louder', but got distracted by something happening in the house, such as being called away for tea. I looked in Christoph's cello part to see if he had a more complete instruction at that point, but it said the same thing: 'sempre' appeared as a stand-alone word. The more I think about it, the more it appeals to me, just to see the single word 'always', without further elucidation. It's not a joke, as it would have been if composer Erik Satie wrote it. Nor is it melancholy, as when the German word 'ewig', with the same meaning 'always', appears in the closing pages of Mahler's 'Das Lied von der Erde'. On the contrary, in the cello sonata it's probably just a little moment of absent-mindedness on Debussy's part which has slipped unnoticed into print. Nevertheless, it gives me a feeling of enlarged possibilities when I reach that point in the movement, and I'm grateful for it.

First-generation musicians

In the music world there are many performers who come from musical families. In those families it is regarded as a great triumph if someone makes a career in music. I have a friend, David Waterman of the Endellion Quartet, whose extremely musical family contains a number of distinguished performers and teachers. When he decided to study philosophy at university, went on to do a doctorate, and seemed as if he was going to become an academic philosopher, his family was a bit disappointed. They were relieved when in due course he saw the light and decided to join a string quartet after all. Needless to say this is very different to the way most families would view the decision to become a quartet player.

What's it like for a musician to come from a background where classical music is regarded as a peculiar thing to do? For a musician there can be many subtle, long-lasting effects from the awareness that other people don't consider music a proper occupation. And yet there must be so many families where a young person strikes out on their own in a pursuit which is unfamiliar to the rest of the family. Indeed, many people who've struck out on their own positively relish the sense of being a pioneer. But to be a performing artist, especially if you are not a natural extrovert, you need constantly to gather up the courage to put yourself on the line, play your heart out in front of strangers, and expose yourself to public criticism every time you appear. It's hard to do so if you suspect that in the eyes of your nearest and dearest you're probably doing something pointless and self-indulgent.

Recently I gave a couple of lessons to a young woman who had just embarked on a music college course as a mature student. She was finally ready to try to live the dream of being a professional pianist. She had always wanted to do this, but her family thought it was just a hobby, not a proper profession. To make this clear to her, her mother used to barge in during her piano practice, speaking over the sound of her playing as though it didn't exist, telling her to come and do something useful, like go to the supermarket or do the ironing. Most musicians, I think, find that when people come into the room when they are practising, the visitor instinctively remains silent and waits until a break in the playing. This was not the case for my student, who understood all too clearly that her playing was interruptible. In that household, playing the piano was seen as a selfish dream which only deprived the household of an extra pair of hands to help with everyday tasks. Not surprisingly, this girl's faith in her musical ability was severely curtailed, and instead of applying to music college she became a secretary. After working in an office throughout her twenties, she gradually built up the confidence to follow her original instincts. Alas, though she's now a good pianist, it was easy to see the damage that her family's lack of belief in her had wrought. She admitted that when she played to other people, she still feared she could not hold their attention.

I was thinking recently about the musician friends to whom I most often confide my thoughts and worries about my profession. It occurred to me that they are all first-generation musicians – that is, the first in their families to become musicians. I didn't know that about them when we first became friends, but it later transpired that we had that important fact in common. We must have observed certain things about one another, picked up certain tones of voice and shades of meaning, which indicated certain shared experiences and made us feel like kindred spirits. Many of us had enjoyed admiration and support from our families, and indeed, many of us benefited from their sacrifices on our behalf. Yet for all of us, there's still a sense that we are 'out there', forging a new path without any advice from those in our families who'd been there before, and often in the teeth of our relatives' misgivings. We first-generation musicians feel drawn to one another, and without wishing to be overly dramatic, I'd say that we all wonder if we have the right to do what we do.

March ...

Round stones

Back in the days when I used to play for the string masterclasses at Prussia Cove, I developed the habit of going for a walk along the beach by myself after the classes, to dispel the tensions of the day. My job was to play the piano for the violinists, viola players or cellists who were having a lesson. The lessons took place in front of a roomful of other gifted students and visiting teachers from all over the world, so the atmosphere was always intense and the stakes high. I wasn't having a lesson myself, but this didn't stop certain teachers from including me in their personal criticisms and tantrums, and I sometimes needed to remind myself afterwards that there were things in life other than music.

I walked slowly along the beach, looking for interesting stones. My method was not to look for anything consciously, but just sweep the beach with my gaze and let the stones call to me. I took them back to my room and kept them on the windowsill as talismans, though I usually liberated them back to the beach before I went home. As I walked on the beach, waiting for 'interesting' ones to present themselves, I realised that I was always drawn to stones which were smooth and round. This may not be most people's idea of interesting stones, but it's mine. I am fascinated by the thought of the multiple forces of wind and water which have to work on a rough piece of rock for years and years to convert it into something smooth and round. Such tremendous forces from so many different directions: what are the chances of them making something round? Far easier to imagine how the clash of asymmetrical forces could produce jagged, dramatic shapes with attention-seeking personalities. There were plenty of those theatrical stones on the beach, but I passed by on another track. I see the round stones as survivors of a long process of buffeting. They hold more secrets.

Playing from memory

I go to a performance of a Bach piano concerto by a young pianist who once came for a lesson with me. I see with interest that he plays his concerto from the score. To me this is striking evidence that the younger generation doesn't feel under quite so much compunction to memorise solo pieces for concert performance. The custom of memorising has come and gone over the past couple of hundred years, and though the fashion has been firmly entrenched for most of my career, I think there's some evidence that it is starting to wane again.

Today everyone thinks that soloists have always played from memory, but it's not true. Even the most famous of pianists, Liszt, appears to have played only half his repertoire from memory. And furthermore, his solo recitals often lasted not more than an hour, not the two hours which recitalists offer today. During concerts Liszt sometimes played with music and sometimes without, putting on and taking off his spectacles accordingly. Clara Schumann told her pupils not to play from memory because it looked like showing-off. Beethoven disliked his pupils playing from memory, because he felt they would forget or ignore his detailed markings. Chopin felt the same, becoming quite angry with students who tried to play his works from memory when they came for lessons. In 1862, Charles Hallé gave a Beethoven sonata cycle in London. He had memorised the works, but found that the public did not like him playing from memory. By the third concert, he had put the score on the music desk and he kept it there for the remainder of the series.

I have a favourite story of Mendelssohn, who had a fantastic memory. Visiting London, he took part in a performance of his own D minor piano trio, but discovered he did not have the piano score. 'Never mind', he told his page-turner, 'just put any piece of music on the desk and turn the pages from time to time, then it need not look as though I play from memory.' Yet by the end of the nineteenth century the fashion had changed, perhaps linked to the fact that improvising in concerts was falling out of fashion. As improvisation disappeared, musicians wanted their playing of composed pieces to look as spontaneous as possible. The public started to expect that soloists would play from memory, and gradually the task of memorising became a daunting part of every would-be soloist's training, a situation which largely prevails today. I was recently on the jury of a competition whose rules stated that everything must be played from memory, even the contemporary piece specially written for the competition, whose composer didn't care in the least whether it was played from memory or not. Some of the competitors told me that they had spent the great majority of their preparation time on the task of memorising the repertoire.

Pianists in their later years often admit to having great trouble with playing from memory, and it's well known that memorising gets harder as time goes on, whether you are a musician or not. The great French pianist Alfred Cortot was well known for memory lapses, and Arthur Rubinstein wrote of his growing dread of playing from memory. Sviatoslav Richter took to performing his recitals from the score by the light of an anglepoise lamp. Clifford Curzon suffered from memory lapses, some of which were caught on recordings. Even Vladimir Horowitz, who in private played a very large repertoire from the score, restricted himself to performing a small number of pieces from memory in public.

There are musicians who memorise easily and feel freer in performance if they play without the notes. But there are

many fine musicians who are handicapped by the unnec-
essary burden of trying to play from memory. The public
today regards it as evidence that the performer has done the
preparatory work, but it should be possible to tell this without
the crude measure of whether the music is on the desk or
not. Today there are leading pianists, such as Pierre-Laurent
Aimard and Kathryn Stott, who play a huge repertoire and
make no apology for using the score. Percy Grainger said
that the ideal would be 'to know the piece from memory, yet
play from the notes'. A friend told me recently that in the
Jewish tradition it's considered important always to use the
text for prayers even if you know the text by heart. There is
always something new to be gained from looking at the text
itself. This certainly seems to chime with the way Beethoven
felt.

Other people's recordings

I sit down to listen to some recordings of other pianists playing Tchaikovsky's *The Seasons*, a set of 12 pieces I'm trying to learn for performance later this year. I had made some headway with them on my own, but was not sure if I was on the right lines. Specifically, I was not sure if I was catching the Russian idiom. So I was hoping for some inspiration.

However, as soon as I heard the other pianists, I felt quite sure they were on the wrong track. They gabbled, they rushed, they treated the piano roughly. The tempos seemed awry; I couldn't imagine what in the music had suggested those tempi to the pianists. The grammar of the music seemed obscure; they didn't sound Russian. Above all, what they seemed to lack was affection – though it's presumptuous of me to say so, as they evidently liked the pieces enough to record them. These recordings were a random sample, but the experience was dispiriting. Or rather, it was dispiriting until I realised that it was also illuminating.

Ravel once advised any would-be composer unsure of his own 'identity' to set out to copy someone else's style. 'You won't be able to', he predicted, 'and in the ways in which you deviate from your model, you will discover yourself.' The same has happened to me. I now feel I know how I want to play the Tchaikovsky.

Actually, I have had one delightful experience of hearing

someone play one of the *Seasons*, but it was only one. When I was on the jury of the Scottish International Piano Competition, we the jury were invited out one evening for supper at the home of one of the organising committee. After supper, several of the jury volunteered to play something on our host's piano by way of thanks. The highlight of this was when the Russian pianist Victoria Postnikova sat down and played Tchaikovsky's 'October'. She played it extremely slowly, far slower than I would have dared to play it myself, and it seemed as if it might have a symbolic meaning. Above her head I imagined a sort of secret bubble with a picture of the Russian landscape inside it. Perhaps also Victoria was drawing on a long Russian performance tradition of which I was unaware. The way she played 'October', it sounded like the essence of autumn melancholy, or more than that, of sorrow and unappeasable nostalgia. It was extraordinarily touching.

For me this experience had a special meaning because when I was a young teenager I remember watching her on television, coming second in the Leeds Piano Competition. My family all thought she should have had the first prize. She was then a willowy and lovely young woman with a soulful expression, and now here I was in someone's living-room with her, forty years later, just a few feet away from her and she had the same soulful look as she played the piano unannounced. I tried afterwards to imagine myself playing this particular piece as slowly as she did it, but couldn't quite see it. As a quick little Celtic person, I might feel like a sheep in wolf's clothing.

$\mathcal{P}$ianist's hands

Arriving in America, you now have to put your hand on an electronic fingerprint reader when you pass immigration control. First one hand, then the other. The immigration official looks at the photos of my fingerprints with some puzzlement. The fingerprints are not clear. He says there must be something wrong with the camera. Can I do it again, first with one hand, then the other? Then he says, 'I don't understand why neither set of prints is clear. The fingerprints are quite worn away on both hands. What hand do you use to write with?' I say I'm right-handed, but also that I am a pianist, and use my hands more or less equally. 'Really? It's unusual for both hands to be so similar. Normally one set of prints is more worn than the other.' I can see he wonders whether I have deliberately done something to evade recognition. My fingerprints refuse to say who I am. It hadn't occurred to me until that moment that the constant touching and stroking of piano keys has actually smoothed away my fingerprints. It suddenly strikes me as funny that something which I do in an effort to give myself identity should actually erase the evidence of that identity in the eyes of security officials.

$\mathcal{P}$redicting happiness

In a political bookshop in Amherst ('making struggle visible since 1976') I come across *Stumbling on Happiness* by Daniel Gilbert, a psychologist and author I haven't heard of before. I buy his book and take it to a bench near Emily Dickinson's house to begin reading in the morning sunshine. It's an enthralling study of psychological experiments to find whether people are good at estimating how happy they will be if certain results come about. It turns out that we are not good at predicting what will make us happy or unhappy, partly because we cannot escape being influenced by the circumstances we are in when asked to make the prediction. Often what people think will make them happy is not the thing which actually does make them happy. And when they look back on experiences, they often recall their state of mind very differently to the way they felt at the time. The teacher they most liked when they were in high school is not the teacher they most appreciate when they think back on their schooldays later. The loss of small things is often felt as more painful than the loss of large ones, and people are less likely to forgive a partner for a minor transgression than for a big one. In short, what we imagine as we look forward is rather different from what we see when we look back. Despite daily experience of trying to forecast our happiness and unhappiness, it seems that human nature constantly wrong-foots us and reminds us that things are more complicated than we realised.

This reminds me of a lovely book I read long ago, *The Snow Leopard* by Peter Matthiessen. The author tells of a journey he made to Nepal in the hope of glimpsing the extremely rare snow leopard, but he never does see it. In the course of his search he meets a wise man who gives him this apparently bleak advice: expect nothing. It doesn't mean much to Matthiessen at the time, but when he later reflects on his outwardly unsuccessful journey, he realises that all his disappointment and frustration arose because of his fixed idea that only a sighting of the leopard would make the journey worthwhile. This expectation is, in fact, the source of the anguish he feels when his goal is not realised. When he turns his mind instead to the wonderful scenery he's seen, the people he's met, the inspiring monasteries he's visited and the things he's discovered about himself, it all seems to have been eminently worthwhile, even if the snow leopard remained out of reach. Like one of Daniel Gilbert's subjects, Matthiessen realises that what he expected would make him happy is not what actually made him happy. 'Expect nothing' is an aphorism he comes to see as full of wisdom.

I've tried to internalise it too, but I often fail. In the life of a travelling musician, where so little is routine and so many new places and situations have to be encountered, I spend a lot of time imagining what they will be like and how I can make the experience pleasant, or at least partially under my control. I seem to have the sort of mind which feels most free in known and stable surroundings. Staring out of my own window at home on a peaceful day I find most conducive to free-floating thoughts, which ironically I'm less likely to have when being flooded with new information and challenged by new circumstances. For me there's some sort of inverse relationship between mental creativity and the nervous stress or excitement of a new location, where I'm entirely occupied with practical matters of where and when and how. In that sense I'm not really cut out for the life of a modern professional musician.

I do find that a positive experience is often directly linked to the efforts I make beforehand to find out about a new place and what it has to offer. Wandering around in ignorance of the fact that the city's loveliest church or most fascinating historical site is round the corner is not something I want to find myself doing. However, I can't deny that my attempts to make the most of a new city often make me anxious and fretful when the places I researched don't live up to my expectations, or turn out to be other than I visualised. Looking back on the visit afterwards, it's often something completely unpredictable that sticks in my mind as the moment when happiness quietly fell on me like snow.

It's easier to experience the truth of 'expect nothing' when you're playing music. In performance, you have to tread the line between knowing what's going to happen (because you've rehearsed it) and being alert to the surprise of it when it does, trying to put yourself in the position of listener who's hearing it for the first time. You have somehow to guide the whole shape of the music but also allow it to be created in front of you. You have to know how to forget as well as how to remember, learning how to embody a curious blend of the knowing and the innocent.

The inescapable mistake

Is it actually possible to practise getting something wrong? On our American concert tour, I notice that night after night, when we reach a certain moment in a Brahms trio where my right hand has to make a big jump from the low to the high treble, I jump slightly too far and land on the crack between two notes. I overshoot by a millimetre or two. After this happens several nights in a row, I start to wonder whether it is in fact 'an accident' on each occasion.

When I have the chance to sit down by myself and take a look at what I'm doing technically, I find that far from making a mistake each night, I seem to have calculated the distance precisely so that I always land on the crack. I have, in fact, successfully practised landing on the wrong note. Yes, it's a big jump, but I could have practised getting it right. Instead, it seems that I have practised getting it wrong. Night after night I can replicate my mistake as though it were a spontaneous event.

Is there, perhaps, something about the emotional meaning of this big jump which makes it feel more 'correct' if there is a touch of over-reaching about it? Have I unconsciously made the jump even bigger so that it feels satisfyingly difficult? It's as though I am unconsciously agreeing with Brahms, 'Yes, this music shows something going too far. And I shall go too far as well!'

I sometimes 'practise wrong notes' in everyday situations too. There are times when I know that what I'm about to say or do is going to annoy someone, but I say it anyway. I could adopt a different strategy and use tact or humour to achieve the result I want, and I greatly admire people who can do that, but to me the 'right notes' of diplomacy don't always feel as if they have the appropriate emotional content.

$\mathcal{N}$ot a building but a sculpture

During my visit to Chicago I have a free day and sign up for a walking tour of downtown Chicago with one of the volunteer 'greeters', local residents who take an interest in the city's history and are willing to escort visitors around some of its sights. My guide turns out to be a charming elderly man in a bow tie. He leads me on an hour's walk around the central area, showing me things that I would never have found for myself, such as an Art Deco ballroom halfway up a high-rise block. He says he's delighted to be showing his city to a visiting musician, and in turn I'm delighted to be shown around by someone who has known Chicago since the days when there were seven railway stations in the downtown area.

When I'm on tour I get quite obsessed with making some kind of human contact with local people; it stops me from feeling like a parasite. My guide points out the differences between buildings of different periods, none earlier than 1900, mentioning that in some of them, the ornamental façade has been coming away from the brick, and that in others the marble cladding has cracked after only a few years and has had to be replaced with granite. Buildings from the 1930s have already had to be restored. All around us, adventurous new buildings are being erected. I don't think I have seen anywhere with such a lust for architecture.

We walk down Michigan Avenue to see the 'Band Shell', a public bandstand designed by Frank Gehry and looking very much like a fragment of his Guggenheim Museum in Bilbao, or like several fragments flung twisting into the air. My guide explains that because of a state law, no buildings may be erected on the lakeside park. However, the Gehry bandstand has been allowed because it 'is not a building, but a work of art'. So how do they define the difference? 'Well,' he says with a smile, 'this isn't a building, you see, it's a sculpture.' What's the difference between a building and a sculpture? 'You can't live in a sculpture, I guess.' But if there's an orchestra and a choir playing inside the band shell, isn't it a building? 'No, because the musicians can't live there,' he beams. 'You can't live in a sculpture.' This reminds me of the legendary Cambridge don who, on learning that he was not allowed to have his cat living in his college room, had the cat registered as a firearm. 'After all, it is a Mauser'.

At the end of our walk I find a coffee shop with an internet café attached, and I write to Bob about the bandstand. I'm still sitting there daydreaming over my coffee when he replies, 'Perhaps a similar concept could be used to get round the licensing laws which forbid groups of musicians to perform in pubs without a licence. Just as the bandstand is not a building but a sculpture, a group of musicians playing in a pub could be defined as a living sculpture which just happens to make a noise.'

A big chip out of the piano

Coming home from playing the Schumann concerto in Grand Rapids, Michigan, I'm feeling rather pleased with myself as I arrive at the airport to check-in for the flight to London. I had worked up to this particular concert for a long time, and it had gone well. I'm even more pleased when a woman recognises me across the airport concourse and comes over to speak to me. She compliments me on the concert, but then asks me whether she could make a comment about the piano.

To my astonishment, she then pulls out of her bag a cutting from the local newspaper. It's the review of my concert, headed by a photo of me at the piano, taken at the performance. The woman points out a) that there is a big chip out of the wood at the corner of the piano, clearly visible in the photo, and b) that the castor-bearing iron frame on which the piano sits was very dirty. 'We were so disappointed by that!' she tells me, with an emphasis leaving me in no doubt that they were. 'I mean, look at that chip! That's not a piano that should be used in a public concert. And the dirt! Does nobody take care of these things? They charge, like, forty dollars for these tickets!'

'And the guy who conducted!' she goes on, warming to her theme. 'He was standing on a little stage that was covered in a kind of indoor-outdoor matting! I mean, what are they thinking? And we were just so disappointed by the way the orchestra was dressed.' At this point I interrupted and said,

'They were smartly dressed!' 'No, they were wearing all kinds of things. Some had pants on, some had dresses, some had velvet, the men had white ties that were not clean. It's not right to make people pay lots of money if they can't even get the orchestra's costumes right.'

I started to defend the orchestra, but suddenly felt over-whelmed by her focus on the non-musical side of a concert I had been proud of. These were things I could have noticed, I suppose, but I hadn't, and even if I had they would have held no significance for me. I could hardly stand the pathetic image of myself absorbed in my Schumann concerto while people in the audience were more intrigued by the appear-ance of the piano. Seeing my face, the woman said, 'I don't mean to take anything away from you. You were dressed real nice. But we'll never forget that big chip out of the piano.'

Trying to claw back a shred of self-respect, I said to her, 'But you must have liked the concert, if you've kept the review in your bag.' She replied, 'I kept it to show our friends. I thought they'd be amazed to see that someone actually put a photo of that piano in the paper.'

Old enough

I was thinking today about the pieces of music that you aren't supposed to tackle until you're 'old enough'. The piano literature contains many examples – late Beethoven and late Schubert in particular. Cellists have taken their lead from Pablo Casals, and usually say that they want to wait until they are forty, fifty, or whatever to play the Bach cello suites in public. In my piano trio, we were nervous about learning Beethoven's 'Archduke Trio' at the start of our time together, leaving it for a few years. String groups feel the same way about Schubert's C major String Quintet, and string quartets about the late Beethoven quartets. I remember a student friend, a very good pianist, saying that he would love to play Mozart's last piano concerto with our college orchestra, but couldn't, because 'nobody would believe me'. Certain pieces of music have a halo of spirituality which is considered to protect them from impertinent assault by people who haven't experienced much of life yet.

A good example of a late work that no teacher would advise a youngster to put in their recital programme is Schubert's B flat Piano Sonata, the last one he wrote. In the nineteenth and early twentieth centuries it wasn't even considered suitable for public performance because of its intimate, meditative character. When it was taken into the repertoire of pianists, it was favoured by intellectual heavyweights such as Arthur Schnabel, Edwin Fischer, Sviatoslav Richter, Maurizio Pollini, Alfred Brendel and Murray Perahia. By the time they had all given us their live and recorded versions, the B flat sonata had acquired an aura of such gravitas that I, in common with many other pianists, did not dare to perform it in public until a couple of decades into my career. I had actually been able to play the sonata since my teenage years, probably quite well, but I never felt able to suggest it for a recital programme until I was much older. By then I don't know if I was actually more able to do it justice, but at least I felt I looked the part.

There's a 'noli me tangere' quality surrounding many famous late works in the eyes of their worshippers, despite the fact that late works are not always extremely difficult to play. Some composers have indeed reserved their most complex music for last, but the late works of others are characterised by a touching simplicity, or perhaps lucidity. It's hard to say which is considered the more daunting, the technical and emotional challenges of a piece like Beethoven's Hammerklavier Piano Sonata, or the alarming minimalism of Schumann's last piano pieces. Mozart's sublime late piano works are restrained in style, and are not technically his most demanding – on the face of it this might make them very suitable for youngsters to play, but few would suggest it, because young people are deemed to lack the necessary maturity. Our current prejudice against hearing these works played by young people is a curious thing when you consider that some of the composers were young men in their early thirties when they composed them. These days it seems rather a waste that we expect young musicians to stay away from certain masterpieces 'until they are ready', because the process of getting to grips with some of these works could actually help to bring that readiness about.

What we seem to like about older players playing great works of music is their air of disarming simplicity. This is generally held to be a quality that has been earned, and is most emphatically not to be acted out by a younger person shrewdly copying the mannerisms of someone who has truly found some peace of mind. Slow tempi have come to be seen as characteristic of an older musician playing a late master-piece, and if a young player adopts such a slow tempo it's perceived to be a cheeky imitation. In fact, the disarming simplicity of older musicians is sometimes encountered in very young players as well, though of course for very different reasons. They and their much older colleagues seem to look at one another from opposite sides of the storm: before and after. Once or twice, when I was head of keyboard at Junior Guildhall, I heard quite remarkable performances by pianists aged about ten or eleven. They were not merely good, but somehow transcendent, and their lack of affectation came across as virtually indistinguishable from the wisdom of old age.

I often wonder if the problem of who may play 'late works' is mostly a visual one. Now that these pieces have acquired their revered patina, it does jar slightly to see a young person performing them, and conversely it seems immediately promising and plausible if a silver-haired performer walks on to the stage to play them. Both of these knee-jerk reactions may be mistaken.

At the International Musicians' Seminars in Prussia Cove, which I attended for many years, there were often very fine performances of masterworks by students in their teens and twenties. In the private atmosphere of those courses, amongst friends, they felt free to tackle whatever pieces they fancied, and they often tackled the 'late works' about which they might have felt inhibited in a more public arena. At the time, I didn't have all that much experience of hearing those works performed by older and more seasoned musicians, but I did realise that many of the students' performances were superb – full of commitment and élan, and often full of understanding too. I still remember vividly a workshop performance of the Schubert String Quintet led by the American violinist Daniel Philips, now of the Orion Quartet. Danny must have been about twenty-five at the time. As the years went by, I had the opportunity to compare his playing of the Quintet's first violin part with that of older, 'wiser' musicians, and frankly I never found any which was more perfectly aligned with the musical content than his was. His young quintet was fired into keeping step with him. It made me realise that there is no simple relationship between youth and immaturity, or between age and maturity. As it turned out, some of those youthful performances were as good as it gets.

Carrying on past the point

When I was a student for a few months in America, I got to know George, an artist who was a friend of my landlord's. During my whole time there, he was working on an oil painting of his grandmother, portrayed as a young woman in a long white Victorian dress. It was fascinating to watch the painting develop. George's grandmother floated up towards us from the depths of the canvas.

The day came when the painting seemed perfect to me, and I expected George to say that it was finished. But he didn't. In fact, he continued painting. First he added whimsical extra colours, and then he added some cosmetic touches to the eyes and mouth. He started painting biographical mementoes in the background. He painted an elaborate border, more eye-catching and colourful than the subject of the portrait, and then he started painting words onto the canvas. The portrait was now a collage in which his grandmother was drowning in a sea of ornamental and historical motifs.

George didn't agree with me about the painting being finished weeks before. I had to accept that its 'perfect moment' was a stage recognised only by me. To the artist, that moment was just another in a long sequence of new ideas he was having day after day. He was embroiled in the process of creativity, addicted to it perhaps. To my eye, his excess of ideas gradually spoiled the portrait, or turned it into something else. I saw his grandmother gradually emerge, become herself and then disappear beneath layers of the artist's personality.

The memory – of watching something sail past the perfect moment – has stayed with me. I often think of it when watching people prepare for a concert, or when preparing for one myself. It's a long process, usually accomplished in a lonely room. Left alone with our thoughts, conscientious musicians sometimes load the music with more ideas than it can bear. Occasionally we lose the ability to see when the subject has come into focus.

When we were just starting out as professional musicians, my violinist friend Krysia Osostowicz and I went to play to one of her old school teachers, Peter Norris, a man whose powers of analysis she valued highly. Afterwards she asked Mr Norris what he had thought of me. 'I love her ideas,' he said, 'only sometimes I wish they wouldn't sound so much like ideas'. Unfortunately, I knew just what he meant. Having ideas about the music was a process we had relished in our rehearsals. But gradually, through experience of performing, I had to learn how to let my ideas sink down into the music and disappear.

April ...

$\mathcal{G}$ardening expert

D.G. Hessayon, the gardening expert who has sold 30 million copies of his books (making him the most successful non-fiction writer ever) was quoted on today's news saying that he doesn't enjoy gardening because he knows so much about it that it is no longer therapeutic.

I often say something similar when people ask if I go to other musicians' concerts for pleasure. There seems to be a fine line between the state of knowledge which allows you to appreciate something immensely, and the state of expertness which means that you know too much to be able to 'suspend disbelief', as they say about theatre. As you acquire that knowledge, listening to other people's performances is more and more satisfying, until suddenly it isn't. Instead of sitting back happily and taking things at face value when you go to a concert, you feel condemned to see the inner workings, the loose threads, all the bits they forgot to include, and often you can't help seeing the hasty welding which has been done at the last minute to make it look like a saleable product. As most of the audience basks in the music, you sit there fuming at the insider knowledge which keeps you at arm's length from true enjoyment.

I wonder if this sense of 'knowing too much' happens more to practitioners than to scholars and observers? Certainly for me at concerts there's a sense of being able to look behind the veil, which means I'm not the innocent listener at whom the performance is aimed. Very few concerts please me thoroughly – though those few are memorable events. I remember a few years ago attending a concert by the Vienna String Sextet. Their chamber music playing was so full of wisdom, tact, gentle determination and middle-European good humour that I felt more and more uplifted during the concert, and went around in a good mood for days afterwards. This was not thoroughly to do with the music itself but with the way they played it – in other words, it was their handling of the music and of each other which pleased me, another practitioner who could imagine how it had all come about, and what ingredients had gone into making that result. On such occasions, I feel that my insider knowledge is a piece of good fortune which equips me to be the happiest person in the audience.

Franchises

Jamie Oliver now runs 'twinned franchises' of his successful London restaurant, Fifteen, in Amsterdam and Melbourne, says the airline magazine. Gary Rhodes now exports *amuse-bouches* to Dublin, Grenada and Dubai. Vineet Bhatia has branched out from his Chelsea restaurant in London to Le Saint Geran in Mauritius. Angela Hartnett, chef at the Connaught in London, is opening several new establishments in the capital this summer and also oversees a resort restaurant in Boca Raton, Florida. Gordon Ramsay's 'empire' now extends from London to New York, Tokyo, Dubai, Prague and now Versailles. 'Can't get a reservation at one of Britain's top-notch restaurants?' says the magazine. 'Try leaving the country.'

But a chef can't be in several restaurants at once, so this is a fiction. Obviously Gordon Ramsay himself cannot cook both at Versailles and in Prague on the same evening, so in what sense is one experiencing his special touch with the food if he's not there? I can only think that he trains other chefs to follow his recipes and then exports them as representatives of his cooking, taking a chunk of the profits because the ideas are his. Why couldn't I learn something from this? I could train young pianists to interpret and play pieces just as I think they should be played, then send them out to play concerts on my behalf, calling them 'Tomes 2', 'Tomes 3' and so on, and taking half the fee because the interpretations are my intellectual property. The Florestan Trio could do the same with a stable of clones disbursing the Florestan brand around the world's music festivals. It seems to me that our recipes for Beethoven and Schubert must be at least as potent as a celebrated chef's recipes for meat and cheese.

Sadly, of course, things are very different in the arts world. We do give out our 'recipes' in the form of coaching and master-classes, but these don't create a brand that can be exploited for our gain. Our ideas pass down the chain and are gone, as of course happens in many educational settings. The recipients of our coaching go off and profit all by themselves (or not), and it doesn't occur to anybody that our investment of ideas and experience should generate a commercial return. Are we in the arts world being very naïve? If people are prepared to pay lots of money to go to 'a Gordon Ramsay restaurant' in Tokyo or Prague, knowing full well that the man himself is in England, why could a pianist not offer, say, 'an Alfred Brendel recital' with AB's approval, disseminating AB's interpretative ideas more widely than he can do himself? There could be bands of pianists all playing recitals simultaneously in Paris, Berlin and Madrid, all exemplifying the Alfred Brendel brand of pianism and making lots of money for its originator. Something must be wrong with this analogy, but I can't quite figure out what. Perhaps food is different because you actually eat it; you feel you've spent your money on something that becomes part of you much more demonstrably than music does, even though the effects of music may be just as long-lasting or profound.

Perhaps I'm wrong in allying the musical performer with the chef, even though there are clearly large elements of perform-ance in a famous chef's public profile. Is a musical score the equivalent of the recipe? If so, the composer must be the chef. Who then is the performer? Performers are somehow cooking from the recipe, eating the dish, but also making it possible for the audience to eat it too.

Whale music

The *Guardian* has rather daringly asked me to review a new book about whale song, which should really be reviewed by a marine biologist, but which seems to stray into my territory. It's daunting to be asked to do something quasi-scientific, as my lack of expertise in this field is well-known to all my friends, but eventually I realise that the best way to approach it is to try and make it interesting for the general reader with fingers in several pies. I try to imagine what I would find interesting myself if I were dipping casually into the book reviews.

A CD of 'whale song' is included with the book, and early in the morning when everyone else is asleep I take it downstairs to listen to it. It's an extraordinary sensation to hear the undersea noises reproduced in my living-room, as though the whales were floating about in the bright English air. Is music the word for the strange basso profundo moans and cries of the whales? Their song has only been known about since it was possible to record underwater. The American navy, listening for submarines, discovered the polyphony of what they called 'biologicals', whales singing in the ocean depths. When the songs were analysed it was found that they had a complex pattern which was sometimes repeated for several hours though it gradually changes, evolving over time. There's nothing like a melody in the sense that we know it. Rather, a series of single utterances like rumblings, wails, cries and even ticking noises.

The book's author, David Rothenberg, points out that speeded-up whale songs sound like birdsong, and slowed-down birdsong (of certain kinds) sounds like whale music. This is a most intriguing idea, though also a frustrating one as we know so little about why. Our own hearing operates in a range which makes us unable to hear the whale's rumbling noises accurately. Rothenberg also says that whales are extraordinarily sensitive to rhythmic change. The pauses between their utterances – like rests in a piece of music – seem important to the structure. All this makes me wonder how I can tell if it's music or not. What would a whale think of my music? I've heard recordings of shrimp which gather in their thousands, making a noise like a tiny electrical static, a delicate crackle and pop. Perhaps that is what my music would sound like to a whale.

The song of the whale certainly has a meaning, one beyond the simple conveying of information about food or females. Why would a creature develop a long and complicated signature tune? It's somehow touching to read that whales sing when they are on their own. It can't be simple echo-location, because that would make the song continuously in need of change. Nor can it be self-expression, because all the whales in the area sing the same song. It may be a kind of song-as-expression-of-time. Can we assume that time passes slowly for creatures who sing a song lasting twenty-three hours? Or that time passes quickly for birds who pack their whole song into a few seconds? Remember that remark about Mozart: 'He didn't die young. He simply went through life at a faster rate.'

Listening to the whale music CD I was struck by one thing which they did seem to have in common with human singers. On old jazz recordings you often hear singers doing a kind of vocal 'flick' upwards in pitch at the end of a phrase. It's nothing to do with the melody, and seems like a spontaneous adornment of the end of the phrase. It's a kind of rapid, quiet glissando lasting only a fraction of a second. Whales seem to do something similar. On the record you can hear them 'yodelling' like this several times in succession in the middle of their songs. I don't know what it means in either case. But perhaps one shouldn't ask what it means, but why it is there.

Tivoli

My trio is in Copenhagen for a concert in the Tivoli Festival. Tivoli is a venerable entertainment park in the centre of the city, with gardens, lakes, restaurants and funfair rides ranging from sweet old-fashioned roundabouts to the latest hair-raising big dippers and machines that rise up and swing children far out into the air above their terrified parents' heads. In the park there's also an enormous concert hall which hosts, among other things, a classical music series which attracts big names. As usual, we're warned that chamber music is often poorly attended.

My dressing room is on the second floor at the edge of the building, overlooking a scene of merriment. A classic car funfair ride is below, a fairytale train ride to the right, a China-town straight ahead with red lanterns bobbing. Above, a big dipper swings by intermittently, passengers screaming in fear and exhilaration. People wander the paths with their baby buggies, eating ice cream and sausages. After standing at my window for a while watching this scene, I go downstairs to take a peep at our audience, nearly invisible and silent in the darkened concert hall. Lights are on on the stage but not above the listeners. Even though it's dark, I can still see that the hall is only about a third full. In strict numerical terms this isn't so bad, as tonight's audience is still probably about the same size as a full Wigmore Hall audience in London, but in this huge hall it looks dispiritingly empty.

Back upstairs in my dressing room, I try to think about
the music I'm going to play this evening – Hummel and
Brahms. It contrasts strongly with the scene outside. I can't
help thinking of the silent respectful audience downstairs and
comparing it with the hedonistic jollity of the surrounding
funfair. I don't like the feeling that I'm a kind of anti-enter-
tainment. At least, I don't want to be the amusement park's
token offering of something virtuous and improving.

The concert hall remains about a third full, and as always
on these occasions, the audience seems to be infected by
the sense of emptiness around them – or so it seems from
the stage. Their response to everything feels muted, and we
find ourselves torn between trying to project our sound as
much as possible into the big hall, and trying to draw them
in instead so that it feels as if they're close to us. Nothing
feels quite comfortable. Leaving the concert hall at the end,
we immediately find ourselves mingling with cheery crowds
flowing towards Tivoli's beer halls and restaurants. People
stare at us, wondering where these formally-dressed people
have appeared from and why they are carrying bouquets and
musical instruments.

$\mathcal{B}$luetooth

In a rehearsal break, my trio colleagues have fun transferring information between their Psion computers using Bluetooth (I'm not very techie and don't have it on any of my gadgets). Information is passed from computer to computer using mobile phones whose 'heads' are pointing towards one another. It seems magical that data can jump from one device to another at my kitchen table in a millisecond.

How useful it would be if we could send data from one person's head to another like that! Often I've wished I could explain to someone, for example, a route I know in the car, just by pressing my forehead against theirs and transferring the knowledge by osmosis. Or how often have I wished, when contemplating my daughter, that I could save her some painful steps to knowledge by simply transmitting the knowledge or experience from my own head into hers, saving her vast amounts of time and heartache.

Perhaps playing music for an audience is something similar to the Bluetooth method. Information is sent in a fraction of a second, passed from brain to brain (the player to the listener) with an immediacy and specificity hard to match. Instead of phones pointing towards one another, we have musical instruments pointing at people's ears and minds. The data 'sent' by music is a very special kind of information not transmissible in any other form, not in text, or numbers, or pictures, graphs or diagrams or spreadsheets. Yet music can make another person feel immediately the information, mood and emotion enshrined in the sound.

Artistic temperament

Today I was chatting to a friend who runs a chamber group. He was complaining how incredibly difficult it is to get any of the members to reply to his questions about their availability for future concerts, or to tell him their feelings about the programmes he has proposed, even though giving concerts is their livelihood. He mails off his suggestions into a silence which is only broken when he summons up the energy to protest. Projects sometimes have to be shelved because of a deafening lack of reaction from the participants – the same people who will say, when they next gather up in the pub, that it's a shame they don't get together more often. 'Ah, well,' he sighed, 'I suppose that's the artistic temperament for you.'

What is 'the artistic temperament'? I've always found this an extremely vexing question, particularly as I don't happen to possess the stereotypical form of it. So often the phrase is used as a synonym for 'a dysfunctional person', meaning someone who can't (or won't) organise their lives, misses deadlines, forgets birthdays, neglects to ask their nearest and dearest how they got on with important stuff, and reacts with unpredictable melodrama to everyday dilemmas. Those with 'artistic temperaments' are perceived to be at their best on the platform, but not the sort of people that you would ask to buy you a pint of milk on the way home and expect them to remember. Undoubtedly in all walks of life there are people highly developed in one particular direction at the expense of

96

the others. And there are also many so self-absorbed that they don't notice anyone else's needs. These types are not confined to the arts, though perhaps it's true that the arts offer them a more forgiving home than other professions do. But even within the arts, there are many other types of people, not given to melodrama, whose whole lives are focused on the arts and who think about music (or words or images) all day long, but who still remember to buy the milk and pick up the dry cleaning.

The public often seems to feel that if there is asymmetry between a person's talent and their capacity to handle the rest of their life, it makes their art more special. But not every artist can thrive in a state of asymmetry. A sensitive artist may feel compelled for their own sake to try and hold everything in balance. They may sense that their artistic side can best be given free rein if it is supported by a stable, functioning self. They try very hard to let their insights percolate through to all parts of their lives because they don't want to grow lop-sided and freakish. Being artistic covers a much broader spectrum than is commonly thought, and it includes many talented people (particularly women in my experience) who may not want to or be able to put on the show of 'having an artistic temperament', but who are artists nonetheless.

$\mathcal{B}$uying another record

Bob is excited to read about the re-issue on CD of a classic Glyndebourne Opera recording of Mozart's *Marriage of Figaro* from the 1960s. We already have this opera on CD, but he says this will be different, a cast with some stars of yester-year, conducted by Silvio Varviso whom he's never heard on disc. We agree that this new recording could be one of his birthday presents.

Later in the day he says, 'By the way, I've decided I don't need another copy of the *Marriage of Figaro*. I don't listen to the one we've got. In fact, I've decided that the version I've got in my head is good enough for me.'

But what is this version? Bob has attended many live performances of the opera and has heard many more on CD. The version in his head must be an amalgam of these, and of the score he's studied and played through on the piano – all now merged into a sort of meta-performance which is probably free of anyone's specific voice or any orchestra's specific sound. The performance in his head is, probably, an imaginary one he can activate at will, detached from any annoying earthly version, free of any real singer's wobbly vibrato or tuning problems, innocent of any real conductor's wilful tempo choices, a kind of Platonic ideal of Figaro.

May ...

Vanished into the ether

In a surge of spring-cleaning zeal I've been clearing out several old fruit crates full of twenty- and thirty-year-old letters I couldn't throw away, but never brought myself to file properly either. They've been lying untouched at the top of a wardrobe. When I get the box down, it looks like some terrible symbolic tableau, envelopes flailing as though stuffed angrily into the box by someone in a passion, yet the impression of rage is choked off by a thick layer of dust.

I look through some of the letters to remind myself what my friends and I wrote so much about. After so long, our ferocious wish to communicate our deepest darkest thoughts to one another seems both striking and sad. We were clearly thrashing about in various nets, wondering who we were, what our relationships said about us, whether we'd ever find someone compatible, how we would ever make our way in the world. We were all so open. Where did we learn that?

These days I rarely write or receive personal letters. I quite often mention my mood in e-mails, but it's years since I sat down to write by hand a thoughtful summary of my emotional state for a friend to peruse at leisure. That's not only because electronic communications are so much easier; it's also because their immediacy has mesmerised us, making a Twitter message sent by someone who is Now, Right This Minute at the top of the Eiffel Tower seem more meaningful than a sheaf of Basildon Bond notepaper dropping onto the doormat a week later with a description of the event. Yet electronic messaging, so easy to delete or to share with many people, is not the right medium for heart-to-hearts. And so it is that the paper trail comes to a sudden stop in the year I learned to use a computer. Since then, most of our bulletins have vanished into the ether.

Those of my friends not in the arts were taken aback when they realised this. For me as a musician, however, it isn't as much of surprise because I long ago had to accept that my most personal utterances disappear immediately. There are recordings, but they're an art-form of their own, very different to live concerts where no microphone is there to make you self-conscious. My favourite bits of playing can never be heard again, or repeated, or stored except in memory. When you're involved in a special performance you feel that you and everyone else will easily remember it. But even I now find that the recollections are melting away. There was always so much emphasis on moving forward, being ahead of the competition, looking to the future, not resting on your laurels. Like Orpheus, we weren't supposed to look back. Trying to remember the details of a particular concert years ago is like being asked what new words your child learned on a given day in the past: you can't recall it, no matter how precious it seemed at the time.

Amateur versus professional

At a party after a concert yesterday, a man said to me, 'I enjoyed reading your book about performing. It gave me a glimpse into a whole different world. I played the violin for about twenty years when I was younger, and I did quite a lot of amateur playing all through those years, but I never came into contact with the kind of experiences you write about. It made me realise what a big gulf there is between the amateur and the professional musician.'

I don't believe there is a big gulf between the amateur and the professional. There are many amateurs who just don't happen to have turned professional, but easily could have done. Indeed, there are many amateurs who have kept their love of music intact because they've never had to confront the peculiar business of trying to earn money from it.

However, across the whole spectrum of music-making there are many different kinds of musicians, and although they may not be divided by whether they are amateur or professional, it sometimes feels as if there are other important distinctions between them. At one end of the spectrum are people who, as Sir Thomas Beecham said, 'may not like music, but they absolutely love the noise it makes.' He was talking about audiences, but there are many players who thrive on the physical sensation of playing, and on the feeling of being plugged into an enjoyable community effort which links everyone through beautiful music. At the other end of the spectrum are musicians who instinctively feel that music is not only a lovely noise but also a portal to something else, something that lies behind the right notes played in the right order. They understand music as symbolic of thoughts and feelings, a vehicle for expressing how the world strikes you.

Sandor Végh used to complain that there was a growing tendency among young players, especially those trained in America, to concentrate on developing a big, beautiful sound with a constant vibrato which they 'poured over everything like a sauce'. He used scornfully to say that their lessons focused on being able to play so loudly that people in the back of the upper gallery could hear every note. The big, luscious sound had become a goal in itself, driving out what Végh saw as the further and more meaningful goal of discovering how to express sorrow, pain and ugliness as well as beauty. He used to warn us that the 'American' type of one-sound-fits-all playing was going to overwhelm older, subtler kinds of approach, and he told us it was our job to resist, to keep it constantly in mind that music is much more than just glamour or loveliness. At the time I didn't listen particularly hard because I hadn't actually come across many of the kind of players he was describing. However, they did indeed become more and more successful and dominant, as he predicted, and there is no denying that the sheer glory of the sound some of them can produce has had a thrilling allure for many listeners.

It now often seems to me that musicians who focus on subtlety and enquiry are made to feel a bit out-dated, a bit 'old European', swimming against the tide of Glorious Sound which is now a priority for many young players. But glorious sound can be completely meaningless when applied to music which is trying to express a whole range of other things.

Words and music

An enjoyable afternoon with the poet James Fenton who has allowed himself to be talked into collaborating with me on a programme of readings to be interspersed with Tchaikovsky's twelve piano pieces known as *The Seasons*. Somewhere in his letters Tchaikovsky makes a remark about poetical words being halfway to music, so I feel he would have approved of our enterprise. I knew from James's writing that he was a great music-lover and renowned for the dramatic rhythm of his poetry readings, so I felt he would be a good partner. James has brought a pile of Russian books, some old, some acquired in a bookshop on the way to my house. He's leafed through them on the journey and has already turned up one or two readings which match the music very well.

He sits on the sofa and reads them to me in his deep resonant voice. I now realise that our joint programme will only work if the music doesn't sound like an illustration of the poem or literary extract that precedes it. It feels much better when the reading is a passage complete in itself, fully-realised, not crying out for sound effects or explanatory background music. If it is a really good piece of writing, it throws a delightful lustre onto the music without either augmenting or diminishing it. The two things stand side by side without propping one another up.

Listening to James and preparing to play, I feel some kind of subtle alteration in the atmosphere, like the way that snow alters the light inside a room. There are some lovely passages – Chekhov on a woman snuggling under the quilt, trying to put off the moment of going to church for the Christmas service, Turgenev on a domestic singing competition where one of the contestants surprises himself as well as the others with the beauty of his voice. These passages stand in no need of musical accompaniment, and somehow this makes them work especially well as the companions of music which needs no literary explanation.

Tchaikovsky's piano pieces are quite tricky, and I've been practising them for weeks in anticipation of this meeting. Yet when I hear James turn experimentally to a passage he's only just come across and 'sight-read' it to me, I'm struck by how quickly one can make prose understood in a convincing and expressive way. Words being our everyday currency of communication, we're naturally geared to making sense of them and extracting meaning from them, even when they are slightly mangled. Occasionally James stumbles over a word, but this doesn't destroy the meaning of the text or break the thread of the narrative; it doesn't strike me as the equivalent of wrong notes in music. By contrast, I suddenly feel very aware of how carefully music needs to be learned and prepared before it can be served up to a listener. I could sight-read my way through unknown bits of Russian music for James's interest, but if I stumbled or hesitated too frequently it would destroy the sense and beauty of the music. Timing, it seems, is more crucial to the coherence of music than it is to speech. The wrong notes of music are more jarring and offensive than little slips in spoken language.

Glimpses of other people's houses

Being a professional musician offers an unlooked-for benefit, the chance to see inside some very exciting houses. In particular, it gives you the chance to sit comfortably in the living-room of the kind of stately homes you would never visit as an ordinary member of the public. It's still the case in the twenty-first century that many concert series are run by, or assisted by, members of the wealthy and aristocratic families who have long been music-lovers and patrons of the arts. Sometimes the concert series take place in their own country houses. It happens quite frequently that we are invited to tea, or for a meal before or after the concert. Sometimes we stay the night too.

As a classical musician you aren't easy to pigeonhole. None of our hosts, it seems, is quite sure whether visiting classical performers are gods or tradesmen, to be let in quietly via the back entrance or welcomed by the butler at the front. We have been treated almost as family by hosts who genuinely enjoy the company of people in the arts. But we've also been offered a sandwich in the back kitchen while the audience was swanning about the grounds with glasses of champagne. I've often been conscious of a sort of delicate probing of our social status. Should they treat us as if we've come to do a job, or as honoured guests bestowing grace on the establishment? If they are music-lovers they mostly plump for the latter, thus allowing us to pretend to be One of Them for the day.

Belonging temporarily to the country house set sometimes makes me feel irritable and frustrated, even when they are being kind and welcoming to us, as they generally are. I can't help thinking it is not good for me to be given these privileged glimpses of another kind of life. Instead of thinking how lucky I am to be having tea in the private drawing-room of Lord and Lady So-and-So, I think dark thoughts about why they, rather than I, should get to live in a castle with a small army of devoted retainers.

It is in these drawing-rooms that I have seen some surprising social gambits which give me an insight into why the castles are inhabited by them and not me. Having dinner at a stately home after a concert some years ago, I found myself seated near a Cabinet Minister who was Minister for the Arts at that time. There had been a savage round of cuts to arts projects, and we had privately decided that whoever found themselves near him at dinner would tackle him on the subject. And so the one of us who drew the short straw asked him what plans he had to protect the artists whose funding had been slashed. His face became inscrutable; he picked up a piece of fruit from the golden bowl in the centre of the table, and studying it as though its features were much more interesting than those of my colleague, he remarked coldly, 'These are very nice apples.' An icy brake had been applied to our discussion.

On another occasion, in another stately home, we were served tea by the wealthy owner, rumoured to have made his fortune via arms dealing in the Middle East. One of my colleagues boldly asked him what work he was engaged in when he lived in the Middle East. Our host stood up, picked up the teapot, looked down on the questioner as if he were about to pour boiling liquid upon his head, and with an intonation worthy of Sir John Gielgud pronounced the line, 'Do you have milk in your tea?' Such ruthless blocking of awkward questions was new to me then, and clearly came from a social armoury of which I knew nothing.

Imaginary Tippex

Sometimes, when I'm writing at my computer, I catch myself in a rather long-winded process of correcting mistakes. If I want to change a word in a phrase or sentence that seems important, I don't just change the word; I delete the whole phrase and type it all again with the new word in place. With really important letters or documents, I might delete a whole paragraph and type it again for the sake of a few words that seem to jar. I feel that if I don't do that, the reader 'will know', even though they clearly won't. There's an element of superstition involved, I admit, and sometimes I feel a bit like the princess in the story of the Princess and the Pea. Yet the effect of the sentence will be different, I think, if my final choice of wording is created on the page in a single, pure sweep of typing. This somehow mirrors the way I hope it will be read: not as a bumpy journey over obstacles, but as a smooth flight. Just changing an unlovable word in the middle of a sentence and leaving the rest intact doesn't give me the feeling of actually having changed the sentence. If I alter a word and read the sentence back to myself, I can feel that changed word bristling. It gives me the kind of feeling I imagine archaeologists must have when they look at the surface of a historical site and know that just beneath the ground are things which tell another story.

It is, of course, needlessly time-consuming to retype whole

sentences when computers make it so easy to change a word without leaving any trace of the old word. Is my habit perhaps left over from the days when I wrote on an old-fashioned mechanical typewriter? We had Tippex to 'white out' mistakes, but as the correction was usually rather obvious, standing out like a tiny dab of brilliant white paint on the paper, we were generally advised to start an important letter again and retype it on a clean sheet of paper. Everyone who used those typewriters will remember vividly the sensation of making an error near the end of the document; there was nothing for it but to tear the paper out of the typewriter, throw it in the bin and start again. Sending out a typed letter with obvious corrections was considered slightly insulting. It's now so easy to word-process a flawless page of typing, but when I started typing letters there was a lot of honest toil involved in producing an irreproachable document.

So in a way I think my habit of correcting whole phrases owes something to my training on an Olivetti typewriter. However, I believe it's also linked to my training as a musician. When you play a wrong note in a musical phrase, there's no point in going back afterwards and banging out the correct note in isolation: 'La! La! La!' The only way to make a meaningful correction is to go back and play the whole phrase again with the right note this time. In fact, it often seems to make even more sense if you take a run at it from much further back in the piece, so that any wrong notes are not only corrected but incorporated into a long sweep of rightness. Corrected in context, and preferably transported along on a big flying carpet of context, the right notes are much more likely to supplant the wrong notes and embed themselves in the memory.

Liking concerts for non-musical reasons

When I attended the wonderful Prussia Cove music seminars in Cornwall, I was always impressed by how many intelligent, creative people volunteered to come and work in the kitchen. For a token fee, but mainly just for the pleasure of living in the special atmosphere, artists, actors, painters, poets and hippies were willing to come and spend several weeks peeling potatoes, chopping carrots and washing up for the hungry musicians.

The music seminars were inspiring events, so it seemed perfectly understandable that artistically-minded people would want to come and help in the kitchen. But I gradually realised that quite a few of them didn't bother to attend the concerts (which for them were free of charge). Nor did they come in to hear masterclasses or rehearsals, even though they had been warmly invited, and although those sessions took place just along the corridor, a few yards from where they sat on the steps with their bowls of peas. When the lessons were over, they crowded round whoever had just been praised to the skies or dragged through the mud, eager to hear what had happened, even though they could easily have been present at the event itself.

Lots of the players had told them they liked the kitchen helpers to come and listen, because it diluted the intense atmosphere and made the musicians feel there was a bit of moral support from people who were not their rivals. But

111

we'd come trooping back from the concerts to find the helpers all listening to rock music in the kitchen. From our perspective, they missed out on the very nub of the matter. Yet they claimed to love being at the music courses, and planed their holidays so that they could do it all again in six months' time. If they weren't interested in the music, what kept them so loyal? All the musicians were bemused by it, yet we accepted that the stimulating atmosphere must have been enjoyable even with the music subtracted. For the kitchen people, the music was a magnet which drew certain kinds of people towards it, and that was what they liked.

A conductor friend of mine recently directed a student orchestra. The concert was a huge success, and many of the players' families came along, bringing siblings and grannies and neighbours. Some weeks afterwards, the conductor was shown a folder of complimentary letters from them. He sat down to read with happy anticipation. But guess what? Not one of the letters mentioned either the conductor or the music itself. Instead, people wrote about the lovely atmosphere, how smart and good-looking the orchestra was, what a great time their young relatives had had socially, and what an achievement to have a full hall. They said the orchestra sounded marvellous and that it was inspiring to see such talented young people playing so well together. They said how glad they were that these young folk were engaged in such a valuable educational activity, and they offered to help in various ways next time. It was clear that they had appreciated the occasion.

Yet the music itself was not mentioned specifically. As my conductor friend said ruefully, he wondered whether all the work and thought that had gone into the interpretation of the works had been worthwhile. He was philosophical about being overlooked personally, but was nevertheless surprised that not one person had written about the music. Is this because people don't know how to put into words their feelings about music, or is it because music is actually in the background for them?

Old expression marks

Some of my printed music scores are now thirty years old or more. Over the years I've written instructions to myself, always in pencil. As time goes by, some of these instructions stay, but others are rubbed out and replaced with new ones. If there's room on the page, I sometimes have several instructions written at different times, with the name or initial of the player on whose behalf I've written them. '"Slow down" (Steven)'. '"Don't slow down" (Christoph)', '"Watch" (Richard)' etc. Sometimes I write things like '"Support violin" (Marieke)' or '"Keep out of way" (Anthony)'. Or it could be the other way round; I'm not suggesting that certain people always ask for certain things. Perhaps the most often used pencil mark is the simple squiggle, a wavy line which alerts me to the fact that the tempo is going to fluctuate for a moment. The fluctuation is generally a dipping below the prevailing speed, creating room to manoeuvre. It can't be defined more precisely than that. Its opposite is the pencilled arrow forwards, indicating that although this is a moment when people generally slow down, we are not going to.

Most of the time there isn't room for multiple versions of the instructions, so my markings of earlier years have mostly been erased. The places which need additional remarks are often transitions between sections, where most players sense that conscious steering of some kind is required. For example, composers almost never indicate that there is to be any let-up in the tempo when the second main theme arrives. Yet players almost always feel that some subtle adjustment is needed at this point, which often marks a change of mood or character. How to get into the second subject is a very common debate; how to play the codas, whether to hasten or delay the very end (the transition into the silence which follows). Sometimes there seem to be many genuine alternatives. Other times I have my own personal favourite way of playing something, but am willing to be flexible. It would be interesting to make a comparative study of all the changes, but my scores are not like a composer's notebooks, later thoughts pasted on top of earlier ones on scraps of paper.

My written remarks are a bit like the passages I used to mark in novels as being especially memorable. Sometimes I look back at a book, see my own pencil marking from teenage years, and can't imagine why I found that passage so scintillating. The lines I underscored now look innocently back at me as if to say, 'Why are you looking at us like that? We don't mean anything.' Again, there are some pencil markings which stand the test of time, while others appear to have been what the Germans call 'Zeitgebunden', the product of that particular time. I've almost given up marking literary passages in pencil now; I've realised that my attention is often caught by lines which reflect my transient preoccupations, and I no longer feel they need to be highlighted in the book forever. No passages have ever been marked in pen.

Out of silence

My friend Greg has given me a copy of a book he loves, *In praise of Shadows* by Japanese novelist Junichiro Tanizaki. The author describes a beloved Japanese culture which, as he points out, is very far from the Western way of perceiving things. He writes of his love of dim light, of shadows, of old materials with natural patina, old silver with tarnish, temples with massive roofs which create banks of shadows underneath. He writes of the beauty of gold statues catching the tiniest ray of light in the dark inner chambers of a temple. He writes of the charm of soft voices, the love of understatement, his abhorrence of brilliant Western lighting which ruins his sense of interacting with the shadows of antiquity.

There's an introduction by Charles Moore of the UCLA School of Architecture, who writes, 'It comes with the thrill of a slap to hear praise of shadows and darkness; so it is when there comes to us the excitement of realising that musicians everywhere make their sounds to capture silence or that architects develop complex shapes just to capture empty space.'

'Musicians make their sounds to capture silence.' Does this strike a chord with me? Not exactly, though of course silence is immensely important. It's the backdrop against which I hope to play, the canvas on which I work, it's the material which runs through the pauses and gaps in the music. Silence is heard in every tiny musical rest. In a way, silence is the very essence of rhythm, because what is rhythm except the organised interaction between sound and silence? Silence is the realm into which any individual note dies away. Yet I could not say I make my sounds to capture it. I can see how, say, a potter might make a bowl to capture a particular shape of air. An architect might design a room which captures light in a certain space. But for me, music does not so much capture silence as sculpt something beautiful out of it. Maybe it is silence that captures music, not the other way round.

June ...

Music chooses you

Sometimes I just feel like learning a new piece for my own pleasure and satisfaction, even if I may never have the chance to perform it. I may not have a clear idea of what I want to learn, but I feel myself getting into a certain mood, and I issue some kind of internal invitation to the right piece of music to make itself known to me.

When I feel the urge to learn something 'random' I get out a whole pile of piano music and play through lots of different pieces, with no conscious agenda. In a way it's like wandering up and down the aisles of a supermarket when I'm hungry, waiting for my appetite to lead me towards one particular foodstuff. Some of the music is enjoyable, some boring, some challenging, and then suddenly – for no immediately obvious reason – one of the pieces will 'snag' my attention in a way different from the others.

It feels almost like a predestined meeting between me and the piece. I sense a need to engage with it, tease it out, puzzle over it. Something in it seems to indicate that over weeks and months of practice it will be a good travelling companion. It might not even be my favourite from among the pieces I looked through, but it feels right in some mysterious way, especially qualified to allow me to tackle some problem I couldn't even put into words. And shortly afterwards I begin the long process of mulling it over. It starts to play in the background of my mind and in the small hours of the night. I play it on table tops. It sinks down into deeper layers of my consciousness, and becomes a kind of mantra on which I meditate. The selection of my new piece is rarely based on conscious choice, but on choice of a kind I don't know how to describe – almost like falling in love on a miniature scale.

The same has happened with books. I've always had a sense of which book would be the right one to read next. And I'm not talking simply about books which seemed as if they'd be topical, entertaining or important, though those are on my reading list too. I mean some kind of recognition that the themes explored in a particular book, or the way they are explored, is significant for me, even though I might not yet know why. The right book often seems to be a little more 'there' on the shelf than the others, if I'm awake enough to notice.

Party frock

A carpenter is coming to build some bookshelves in the bedroom, and in preparation, I move some stuff out of the way into the wardrobe, slotting the ironing board in at the side. I find myself pushing out of the way a pink velvet party frock, made by my mother, which I wore as a child. Its style is not one that would suit today's children, but I couldn't bring myself to get rid of it. Seeing it there reminds me of how, when we had visitors, I used to dread the moment the call went up: 'Susan, come and play your piece!'

I was a very shy child and the effort involved in playing to other people was enormous. However, I admit that their pleasure in what I played was a chance to break through the barrier created by shyness and attain sudden (if brief) success. Much as I desperately hoped to be left alone and not called to perform, I also felt boosted by our visitors' appreciation – though not so much that I would actually have volunteered to play without being asked. These mixed feelings have persisted to this day. After many years in the profession it sounds absurd to say this, but I've never quite come to terms with the public nature of being a performer. I recognise that I'm good at what I do and that I have earned my place on a concert platform. I'm not a fraud; I take my responsibility to the audience seriously. Secret shame and guilt are not ingredients in my mental state. I don't have doubts about my ability, and I have plenty to say about the works I love. I value the audience's appreciation hugely. However, even when I'm particularly looking forward to a concert, I still have an equal and opposite desire to be left alone and not have to do it. This resistance reaches its peak in the hours before a performance, when I often feel almost sleepy and indifferent, my mind perversely and obstinately turning on all kinds of matters completely unrelated to music. I often spend the last hour before a concert wishing that I was sitting by the fire instead. There's even a feeling which sometimes creeps up on me shortly before the concert, a curious sense that I have already done it, and can stop thinking about it now. Rationally I know quite well I have not done it, but nevertheless I experience a subtle conviction that the performance has already taken place. I think this is something to do with mental effort which reaches a kind of saturation point, making one feel suddenly disgusted by the idea of more.

Many performers have struggled with these ambivalent feelings – think of all the stories of great artists feeling sick in the dressing room, and having to be pushed on stage by their assistants. There must be many people who fall into the profession because they happen to be good musicians, and of course one gets trapped into the cycle of needing to earn money. But being a good musician doesn't necessarily mean that one has the stomach for the pressures of being a performer. Innate talent doesn't always go hand in hand with having the kind of nervous system which can easily cope with public scrutiny, but I guess many people, parents as well as gifted young musicians, believe that the one will naturally lead to the other. For some, it does: I have plenty of colleagues who can't get enough of the limelight and are never happier than when scenting the air of a concert hall.

I also like to be appreciated; it often feels like the only pay-off for all the days, weeks and months spent in solitary practice. I love the audience, but I have a love–hate relationship with the act of performance. My mind likes it, but my body doesn't, as I realise every time I have a painful abdominal cramp before or during a concert. When I used the phrase 'one doesn't necessarily have the stomach to be a performer', I meant it quite literally. There's certainly something that keeps me going, and it may go right back to that early experience of live performance enabling me to burst through the barriers erected by intense shyness. The party frock in my wardrobe is a reminder of the long tussle I've had with myself about whether nature has really cut me out to be a performer.

*D*ice games

Bob has been devising some musical games for students on a music course, and he reminded me that even Mozart had joined in a late-eighteenth-century craze for 'musical dice games' by publishing minuets made up of tiny numbered units that could be assembled by the player in various orders according to the throw of a dice. Such pieces are never very interesting, because the little units need to be bland enough to fit with the others in whatever order they land up. Nevertheless the dice games must have given the players a feeling of being musically creative in a small way.

I think I've encountered the present-day version of dice games several times this year when invited to listen to musical tracks put together on computer by teenagers of my acquaintance. They too used pre-supplied units of music, easy to find in very sophisticated packages which enable them to produce within a few clicks and a bit of cutting and pasting a very plausible piece of electronic pop music. Even people who can't sing, read music or play an instrument can easily learn to assemble something in the popular style of the time, using material supplied by someone else.

There is nothing wrong with using the style of the time, of course. Indeed, I often envy Mozart and his contemporaries because in their day it was natural to write in the musical language which everyone shared. There was none of the obsession with Originality that we've come to feel in our own era, when for example artists feel under pressure to come up with no more than a novel concept, abandoning traditional ideas of beauty and self-expression. In that sense I think it's a good thing that people can have a go at assembling a piece of music from ingredients they recognize from music they play every day on their i-Pods. It gives the welcome feeling of a lingua franca amongst music-lovers.

However, it also makes me feel slightly uneasy. There's a big difference between the musical dice games of the eighteenth century and the identikit 'songs' of today's teenagers: the dice games were understood by everybody as games, whereas today's youngsters are encouraged to think that assembling musical units amounts to real composition. For me, such pieces remain musically inert unless I can sense that the composer's brain has done something creative with the musical material. I want to feel that he or she has thought about it, made links between things, and created something more than the sum of its parts. When this happens, music comes alive. When it doesn't, this kind of activity is more like putting a bunch of plastic flowers in a vase and thinking you now know how to grow things.

Turning up the volume

At the end of a day of rehearsal, my hands often ache, and sometimes they're still gently aching when I'm lying in bed. As I think back on the day's work, I seem to hear all the requests to play louder. 'It doesn't really sound fortissimo.' 'That doesn't really sound like an accent.' 'Don't you have "marcato" there? It doesn't sound like it.' 'I know it says "quiet" but it has to be a really *projecting* quiet!' 'The bass isn't nearly loud enough.' 'Can you really bash out that line?' Sometimes the feeling of pounding the piano keys becomes quite unpleasant, as though the little bones of my hands are being jarred.

I'm sure that the volume level at which we play has risen over the years, but I am not sure why. It isn't conscious; we never said to each other, 'Let's play louder this year', but somehow it has crept up on us. I'm certain my hands didn't use to feel this way after a long rehearsal, like lemons that have been squeezed dry. Concert halls, of course, are larger than they were when most of our favourite works were written – and of course a lot of those works weren't designed to be played in a big hall in the first place – but the size of concert halls has not really changed over the course of my career. Instruments may have become more powerful – modern concert grand pianos have a more penetrating tone, and string instruments have been modified and fitted with special strings to maximise their carrying power. But I think the blame for the rising volume level lies with the wholesale use of amplification for most kinds of music other than classical.

In the last couple of decades, there's been a big and to me inexplicable rise in volume at pop and rock concerts, to the point where the decibel level of certain bands is often proudly mentioned as if it were an artistic quality in itself. Everyone has got used to hearing music at a volume greater than human hands or voices can produce. There's something unnatural about this, and I profoundly hope the taste for it will gradually ebb away. We have increasing evidence that loud music causes hearing damage, but so far, both musicians and fans seem amazingly cavalier about it – except for the few who've gone public with their regrets about tinnitus and hearing loss.

In the meantime, we've all been infected by the feeling that music should be loud, even in classical music where amplification has never been routinely used. Because of amplification in the pop world, people have become accustomed to seeing musicians play their instruments with minimal effort but maximal volume. This is dangerous for those of us who seek to achieve a powerful effect with physical means alone. We're very conscious that on stage we can seem tiny and remote, like people viewed through the wrong end of a telescope. Anthony recently commented to me that if it were not for the constant technical study of how to produce a really carrying tone for large halls, his violin practice could be reduced to a fraction of its amount. This seems sad to me. If we could jump back in time and listen to a performance by, say, Schubert's friends or Beethoven's favourite quartet, I'm sure we'd find them playing at a more intimate sound level – yet clearly the expressive effect of the music was as great for listeners who were attuned to those levels. What would musicians of the past think if they heard us all moaning about our aching hands and sore shoulders at the end of rehearsals? I know I play more loudly than I used to, though it's not because I want to. Somehow the volume level has been gradually turned up by an invisible hand.

$\mathcal{K}$eyboard touch

It's often said that the piano is a glorified percussion instrument, and that it can't make a smooth, singing sound. As you strike each note, the sound begins to die immediately. It's impossible to create a truly sustained line out of a series of notes which lose strength from the instant they're struck. But you only have to listen to a selection of different pianists to know that some of them can certainly create the illusion of a singing tone on the piano. In part this is created by finger legato, partly by the sustaining pedal, and partly by a very subtle management of other voices underneath or on top of the singing line so that it appears to hang in the air. By this means a single melody note can even seem to grow louder rather than dying away.

I was watching my own hands on the keyboard this afternoon, and I suddenly realised that I had completely lost sight of the fact that the sound does not come out of the keys. When I touch the keys I imagine that sound is created directly underneath my fingers. Rationally, I know that the key is only the starting point of a long lever and series of joints. When I press down the key, I set in motion a sequence of mechanical movements which results in the felt-covered hammer striking the string a couple of feet away from me, in the interior of the piano. But it doesn't feel like that. I have somehow managed to 'forget' that the sound is produced a little distance away, and is not actually created at the point where my finger meets the key surface. In my mind the key and the actual striking-point have coalesced and are one and the same.

With one part of my brain I know this is very silly of me, but I also feel that my wilful misunderstanding may have an important purpose. It certainly has an enormous influence on the way I touch the keys. If I always bore in mind that I was only pressing down the end of a lever, an inert piece of wood, I would not see the point of touching it with great care and affection. As it is, my feeling that the keys are capable of responding to very subtle shades of touch is the source of my particular piano sound. I feel that I am coaxing a singing sound out of the keys themselves, and even if this is nonsense it definitely helps me to produce the sound I'm after. Sometimes, when I listen to other pianists, I can tell from watching their hands on the piano that they know perfectly well the keys are only levers. This is not to say that they don't have supreme control, but the relationship between mind, hand and key is different. These pianists may well be throwing their imaginations forward to the point where the hammer strikes the string, controlling that process remotely from their vantage point at the end of the lever. But even if this is the accurate way to conceive of how sound is made on the piano, I don't find it helpful to think of it that way. It feels more fruitful to imagine that you can stroke a singing tone out of the keys themselves, and have them sing back at you.

$\mathcal{T}$he end has been known for 150 years

Today the *Guardian* has asked several of its sports writers to attend arts events and write about them as if they were arts critics. One of them, golf correspondent Lawrence Donegan, goes to an orchestral concert featuring a performance of Brahms' first piano concerto, with the American pianist Yefim Bronfman as the soloist.

Though Donegan was impressed by the skill and the sound of the playing, he is not ultimately gripped by the performance, and asks himself why not. He concludes it's because it is so unlike a sports match, where the excitement lies in the fact that the outcome cannot be known in advance. You don't know which side will win. In contrast, he realises that the whole course (and the ending) of Brahms's first piano concerto 'is known, has been known for 150 years, and isn't going to change in the next 150'. This makes it unexciting for him, and he can't quite imagine how people can be so enthusiastic about something whose ending is known – indeed committed to memory long ago by many of the audience. I wonder if he would say the same thing about, say, Shakespeare's *Hamlet*? Would he even like it if his favourite song had a different ending next time?

It's interesting to think about the attitude of someone who finds a musical performance dull because the composer has already plotted the course of the music. I'm aware that the composer has done so, too, but for me the interest lies in how the musicians plot their own journey through that landscape delineated by the composer. If the ending were unknown, their collective energies would have to function in a completely different way, more as they do in improvisation – which in my experience is a lot of fun, but never so fulfilling. The satisfaction of 'reading' the landscape together, arriving at the North Pole together (as it were), would be impossible. I feel there's an important insight lurking here about the approach needed to enjoy classical music – indeed serious art of any kind – though I can't quite put my finger on it.

The 'unknown outcome' of sport often seems a shallow reward when you watch a game that seems almost randomly won by one player rather than another. How often have I watched a very close match and felt it was a shame that one of two superb players had to prevail at the last moment? Even when the match has been close and wonderfully played by both from start to finish, such a gulf opens up between 'the victor' and 'the loser' as soon as the final score is posted. One gets to hold the trophy aloft while the other sits forlornly in the shadows, though just a moment before they both seemed equally worthy, equally capable of victory. This gulf often seems completely unjustifiable, a theatrical convention which has more to do with commerce than with what I saw during the match. Though I can see that the struggle to prevail brings out the best in many sportsmen, the fact that one of them wins is, for me, hardly the point.

$\mathcal{F}$ederer v. $\mathcal{N}$adal

I spent most of the afternoon and evening watching the 2008 men's tennis final at Wimbledon between Roger Federer (the reigning champion) and Rafael Nadal. It was an epic five-set match of fantastic quality which started at about 2.30pm after a rain delay, and finished, after several more rain delays, at about 9.30pm when it was almost too dark to see the ball.

Afterwards, Bob and I reminisced about our attempts to learn tennis when we were young. I told him that my sisters and I used to go down to the public tennis courts in Portobello near my home in Edinburgh. We had probably never seen a professional tennis match, or indeed any sort of tennis match; we just knew that tennis was about hitting the ball to and fro across the net with a racquet. We had a few lessons and became quite good at leisurely rallies, hitting the ball casually back and forth across the net without any attempt at speed. Sometimes we could keep our rallies going for quite a long time, and I found this enjoyable. During our long rallies I found myself happily thinking about other things, my mind engaged in some unspooling daydream while my physical self engaged in the act of running and hitting the ball. It was a pleasing combination.

Then our tennis teacher explained that we should now learn to play 'properly'. It was only then that I realised we were meant to hit the ball in such a way that the other person could *not* hit it back. This came as an unpleasant surprise. As soon as we started 'playing properly', our points became extremely short. One person served, the other could not hit it back, and that was the end of the point. Instead of being immersed in the pleasing swing of the ball back and forth across the net, we now spent most of our time running to the far corners of the court to retrieve the ball after it had rolled away out of our reach. This was much less fun.

It seemed to me that there was equal skill in hitting the ball so that the other person *could* hit it back. If they could, the ball would flow, one got to move about and there was not much interruption to the rhythm of play. It struck me that hitting the ball deliberately out of the other person's reach was very unsportsmanlike.

When I tell Bob all this, he's very amused and says, 'There speaks a true chamber musician.'

$\mathcal{R}$emembering $\mathcal{G}$yörgy $\mathcal{S}$ebök

A pianist is coming over from Belgium this week to have a lesson with me. Just thinking of the effort involved in arranging flights and somewhere to stay in London, I feel very responsible for the success of her visit. I usually experience some insecurity before teaching anyone, though the feeling has gradually diminished as I have accepted that I do have useful things to say, things my students cannot know yet because they have so little experience of performing these pieces to all kinds of different audiences.

There are lots of theories about the best way to teach, but it's hard to know how to relate them to music, where 'the goal' and 'the learning outcome' seems to vary from person to person and piece to piece. Thinking back on it, I don't believe that any of my most helpful teachers emerged from an orthodox training course, and indeed their methods might have been frowned upon in such courses. I haven't been trained to teach, either, but I cling to the feeling that I may have useful knowledge to pass on, and I even feel it's unlikely to be passed on if I follow a step-by-step learning model. So often with advanced students of music one has to jump several steps ahead, approach from the side, or contradict things you said earlier. These gambits are made not with conscious design, but when they seem right, and who can teach you that? The music itself, which of course varies from lesson to lesson depending

134

on what the student brings, is the territory through which we try to find paths, factoring in what Jeeves would call 'the psychology of the individual'. There's no 'standard method' for this, nor could there be.

I still have not seen the instinctive method better demonstrated than by the Hungarian piano teacher György Sebök, who once told me at his summer course in Switzerland that he tried to empty his mind before listening to each student, and begin the lesson with no preconceptions about what they might do, or how it might strike him. This is awfully hard to do, unless you are supremely tranquil about your own abilities, as he was. I've tried his method, and I find that if I manage to let go of any ideas about how I hope my student will play, then I also lose the will to steer them in one direction rather than another. Emptying my mind seems to make me merely absorbed in whatever the student does, with no desire to persuade them that it could be done otherwise. 'Ah, so they're playing it like that. How interesting!' I feel myself think. And that is the end of that. My sense of critical judgement has gone, and with it the desire to teach. For Sebök it didn't seem to be like that. He claimed that what interested him was the gap between how the student played and how they would ideally *like* to play. His interest was in helping them to close that gap.

The last time I heard Sebök teach, I travelled to Utrecht to listen to some of his Liszt masterclasses, which attracted a large and worshipful audience. I didn't play in the class myself, because I've never been particularly drawn to learn Liszt's music. However, it was fun watching other people play it, and at one point Sebök did one of his party tricks. He was listening to an Italian girl he had never met before. She was playing one of the Liszt 'Sonnets', a virtuoso piece. She played technically very well, but something about her playing obviously puzzled him. He leaned forward intently as she played, his arms dangling loosely at his sides in his curious wise-monkey fashion. When she had finished, he asked her to please go and stand a little distance away, where she could not see the piano keys. Then he sat down at the piano, played her a single note in the middle of the keyboard, and asked her to sing it back to him. She couldn't. He played her a few other notes, all easily within her range, but her guesses were wide of the mark; she sang much too high or low, and her singing had the strange faltering quality of those who are tone deaf. The audience gasped, and the girl herself was stunned. 'How did you know …?' she managed to say. Sebök said nothing, but he smiled and tapped the side of his nose, as if to say, 'I smelled it.' This was not kind, but it was terribly revealing, and at the time seemed almost like magic – black magic perhaps.

Could I have smelled what he smelled? All I consciously noticed at the time was that she did not seem to be sensitive to the different keys through which Liszt's very chromatic harmonies were passing. Her tone colour, her body language and facial expression did not change as she went from key to key. Perhaps this was all that Sebok had noticed too, but he had much more confidence to interpret it as a sign of something bigger. Exposing her like that was a daring tactic, one that was very un-British. But teaching is not always a matter of being kind, and I was learning that there were many ways to open a student's eyes.

At the end of the masterclasses there was a question and answer session for the listeners. I stood up in the stalls and asked Sebök how he knew which direction to go in with a student if he had emptied his mind of preconceptions. His answer was drowned out by the burst of offended muttering which broke out all around me as his fans registered my disrespectful question. He said something like 'It's not always important to know the goal in advance', but his words were muffled, and I never had the chance to ask him again.

Stuck

Learning a piece of music has a strange curve, not at all consistent. In a way it is nothing to do with conscientious practice, or at least it isn't predictably yoked to that. For weeks now I have felt 'stuck' with the Mendelssohn variations I'm currently practising – the *Variations Sérieuses*. Though I have tried all my own practising advice on myself, I seem to go day after day at the piano without making any progress – or at least, the progress is so slight that I can point to individual bars and beats and locate my progress within a tiny area. I learned how to jump to a certain chord without hitting a stray note on the way, or something like that. Apart from that, there seems to be no wind in the sails.

Yet I know from experience that this is not the end of the story. Very often there's a plateau of immobility which a player has to live on for a while before something else can emerge. It certainly isn't due to lack of effort on my part, but seems to be linked to other lines and curves on other graphs which are not under my control. I know that if I keep at it, sooner or later will come a day when I sit down in the same way and play the same notes, but suddenly find that I have taken a step up in my level of accomplishment. It's like pushing against a heavy door which suddenly opens. Things will seem technically easier, structurally clearer, or in some mysterious way will seem to have sunk down (or risen up) into a mental layer where less conscious effort is needed. I will suddenly feel like a better pianist. This can't be hurried, unfortunately. And it probably won't happen if I don't become fed up with my stuck-ness in the first place.

Recently a friend of mine, a prize-winning poet, told me that he felt he had reached a similar plateau with his poems. He said they were as deep as he knew how to make them. We were walking through St James's Park on a sunny afternoon. People were sunbathing and kissing in the grass all around us, a cheerful scene which formed a strange backdrop to our conversation as he earnestly said, 'I would like to go deeper, but I don't know how. How does one go deeper?'

People don't often voice thoughts like this, so I was very touched, but didn't have any answer except to say that the desire to go deeper is surely the gate which will eventually swing open. At the same time, I suspect that even without the desire, life sometimes comes along and swings open the gate whether you want it or not.

July ...

Unreturnable balls

On holiday in a little Italian hilltop town where a masterclass is going on, taught by a visiting Russian piano professor, we attend the final concert in a room of the palazzo.

Six different pianists perform virtuosic piano music, but they might as well be only one person, so similar are their styles. During the undigested torrents of arpeggios, I think of Barenboim's remark that a musician must know how to group notes. A simple observation, but how much lies behind it! These pianists seem to be ignorant of it. They all have the same faults – at least to my Western European ear. They love to punch out chords so forcefully that it reminds me of a tennis player slamming down an ace, exulting in the fact that it's unreturnable. It makes me wonder what they think artistic power really is. The power to deafen and startle the audience? I feel myself jumping in my seat each time a loud chord is struck (and I mean struck). Bent over the keyboard with grim expressions, there's a hint of Charles Schulz's cartoon strip 'Charlie Brown' where Schroeder hunches fervently over his tiny piano with the bust of Beethoven on the lid.

With this continually loud playing there is no perspective, no layers of light and shade, and far from seeming continuously impressive, it only seems monotonous. Where is grace, humour, humanity? I wonder what they've been talking about all week in their masterclasses. Is this the way they want to play, and do they realise how similar they all seem?

After over an hour of Liszt, Busoni, Schumann and Chopin, I feel I haven't heard a single beautiful piano sound, let alone a passage of ravishing quiet playing. And least of all have I heard the sort of personal speaking tone, finely graded, which would identify a particular player and let me glimpse their inner self. The phrase 'épater le bourgeois' comes to mind as I listen. This is piano playing as intimidation – and most annoyingly of all, the audience seems pleased to have been intimidated, as audiences often are by domineering pianists. They shout 'Bravo!' as I fume inwardly.

Community opera

Under a full moon, on the cathedral steps of a little Italian town, the local dramatic society performs its annual musical drama one evening. It's a historical play with a large cast in medieval costume and a live orchestra in a sort of sheep pen between the open-air audience and the stage. Libretto and music have both been freshly composed, following an old pattern. The libretto is supplied in the programme book, and I'm surprised to see that the whole text is divided into little chunks of four lines each, rotating more or less equally between about eight principal characters.

As the opera gets under way, we realise that each character has been allotted his or her own unique 'song', to which all their verses are sung. Some people's songs are cheery, some are stern and manly, some are lyric. Each person's verse is preceded by a sort of wake-up call from the orchestra, a jaunty little rhythmic signal designed to alert each singer to the re-appearance of his or her music. The effect is unintentionally hilarious. As the plot develops, the songs remain obstinately the same, each character stepping forward to reprise his usual melody, but with words appropriate to the unfolding plot. The story unfolds but the music remains exactly the same, so that as the climax is reached with the heroine being stabbed and the scheming prelate finally arrested and imprisoned in the cardboard tower, these dramatic happenings are relayed in the same four-line ditties we'd heard at the beginning.

There's a kind of ludicrous tension between the non-developing music and the increasingly dramatic plot, and in fact the yawning gulf between the two makes us feel quite hysterical as the night wears on. Maya said it made her think that if the young Mozart had stumbled on such a performance on one of his trips to Italy, he must have thought, 'Good Lord – fetch me some paper and a pen. I can do better than this!' Sitting through this opera is a very good instant composition lesson in why music has to develop when it tells a story. It's the first time I've ever heard a musical drama where the basic building blocks of music were innocently deployed with no thought of their dramatic context. Perhaps it is done for practical reasons. Very likely the only way to rehearse a long opera with a big cast of amateurs is to allot each one a song of his/her own and a bunch of verses, or texts, to learn to that same music. Then you assemble the cast, inform them of the order in which they sing, and off you go. Not one of these performers is a trained singer, and curiously this has a pleasing effect. They strive to sing loudly and firmly, but there's no showing off and nothing to show off about. The overall effect is simple and touching, making us feel we've glimpsed a folkloric community effort which must have changed very little over decades or even centuries.

$\mathcal{D}iving$

Returning from holiday and trying to play the piano is always horrendous. My fingers feel like sausages. They don't seem to flex in the right places any more, and I know from experience that this will last for a while; I will have to work my way patiently through limbering-up exercises and slow practice, all of which will make me feel ten years old again. So instead of addressing myself to this task, I watch Olympic diving from Beijing on TV. As often with high-quality sport, my attention is drawn by something I can scarcely put a finger on. Diver after diver performs a difficult dive, well executed. All of them look composed and purposeful as the camera lingers on their faces in the moments before their dive. They're all so accomplished, and in a way there seems very little difference between them.

Yet with most of them, you remain aware that you are watching a difficult thing, well performed. The concept of 'difficult thing' remains uppermost in your mind even as you admire their dedication and skill. With a few of them, however, the difficulty seems to vanish; you're only aware of something beautiful occurring with a sort of transcendent naturalness. Obviously these few divers have undergone the same arduous training and the same steps towards mastery as all the rest. They must be just as scared or nervous as they stand on the board. But there seems a qualitative difference between the two kinds of divers, the high achievers and the poets. How is the extra step taken, the step which makes the adjective 'difficult' vanish from the spectators' minds? As soon as I see the Chinese girl who eventually wins the women's gold medal, I know it's going to be her. Whippet-thin and as keen as a blade, she flashes through the air like a shooting star, not a human being. She has clearly reached some place in her mind where the dive is a single thing, not merely a handstand followed by half-turn, three somersaults and a pike.

I've noticed the same when watching ballet and other forms of dance. There are dancers who can somehow link a sequence of moves into something which transcends the individual steps to become a whole phrase or sentence. The secret seems to lie in the ability to connect. Instead of one movement followed by another, you see an over-arching meaningful 'melody' of linked movements. As with beautifully played music, the transitions are never awkward, but become delicate hinges allowing one movement to blend into the next. And indeed, the transitions themselves become meaningful and touching, instead of the awkward little punctuations they can be in the hands (or feet) of a less poetical dancer. What separates the merely skilful from the 'musical' dancer is impossible for the non-specialist to analyse, and I imagine is very difficult to teach, but you know it when you see it. It must be each dancer's own secret discovery.

All this intrigues me because of the analogies with getting music ready for performance. When I watch these athletes and dancers, I recognise that in their own field they are confronting the same boundaries between being good and being excellent. Just as the diver has to roll all the individual movements into one smooth arc, the musician learning a piece has to join up all the dots, grouping them into patterns and gestures which make a larger kind of sense.

Not enough of a charlatan

Walking on Wimbledon Common in the sunshine today, Bob and I were talking about singers and pianists. We came to talk about pianist Graham Johnson, the mastermind of Hyperion's Complete Schubert Edition, on which he played the piano with all the singers in 600 songs and wrote all the sleeve notes, later turned into a book. I was telling Bob that twenty years ago or more, Graham came to hear me at the Wigmore Hall. Afterwards he popped backstage and said to me with a twinkle, 'If I may say so, my dear, you are not enough of a charlatan.' I was slightly crushed by this remark, and for ages afterwards I fretted over it from time to time, wondering if my stage manner was too plain.

Bob listened to this tale with some surprise and then said, 'But you do know it was a quote?' I said I didn't know it was a quote. Then Bob explained that a singer named Vogl had made the comment when he first met Schubert and heard him play the piano. Vogl was considerably older than Schubert, and was nearing the end of a successful career as an opera singer. Later, he and Schubert became firm friends and often gave the first performances of Schubert's songs together. Vogl came to appreciate Schubert's lack of affectation and see it for what it was. His earlier, rather pompous remark, 'You are too little of an actor and not enough of a charlatan' has gone down in music history. Hearing this explanation, I suddenly realise that what seemed like a criticism from Graham was perhaps a gracefully lobbed compliment dropping too close to the net for me to catch it. How many remarks addressed to us by other people do we store in our brains for years for entirely the wrong reasons?

After-concert nodding and smiling

Today I went to an excellent lunchtime concert in Cadogan Hall, part of the Proms Chamber Music Series. I knew several of the players, so afterwards I went round to congratulate them on their performance. I don't very often go to other people's concerts, so normally my experience of after-concert conversations is confined to me, a performer, receiving other people's comments.

As a member of the audience myself, I was struck today by the peculiar behaviour of the players, who were exactly as I feel I am myself after concerts. Still dazed by adrenalin and by the effort of their performance, they were wreathed in ridiculously fervent smiles, greeting their admirers with a relief and exhaustion that found expression in maniacal nodding and grinning, quite different from their composed and serious selves on stage. Torn, as performers always are, between agreeing that they were very good, and trying to retain a modicum of self-effacing restraint, no sensible word came out of anyone's mouth except for 'Thank you, Thank you', 'I'm glad you came', 'Thank you, yes, we were pleased with it too'. I knew exactly how they felt, and still it struck me as a mixture of touching and dysfunctional. As I watched them playing, I had felt I knew what each of them was like (serious, dedicated, almost grave), but afterwards it seemed as if they had each imbibed a bottle of champagne between leaving the stage and arriving in the foyer. The atmosphere was frothy and buoyant, almost puzzlingly so if you didn't know something about the effects of adrenalin.

People who don't perform themselves have little idea of how live concert performance deranges you slightly. Even musicians who are very well prepared, and able to perform confidently, are still de-railed by the experience. For a while afterwards, they still feel slightly drunk from the sensation of putting themselves in front of the public and doing something difficult which calls on unusual reserves of emotion, strength and concentration. Directly after the concert, they're still in the grip of performance energy, still rocked by the audience's reaction. So often I have waited backstage for the first audience members to come and say hallo, my heart still beating fast from the effort of the concert, cheeks burning, my smile helplessly exaggerated as though I can't keep my facial muscles under control. People come and speak to me and I realise I am staring deep into their eyes, even though I don't mean to. Staring deep into people's eyes is really not one of my things, but it feels as though my vision has been augmented to laser-sharp clarity by the experience of live performance. There is something about the intensity of the music-making which still burns within us, like a fire that remains hot for a while after everyone has left the room.

Ending in forty seconds

I quite often see my daughter at her computer listening to downloaded music whose course is being measured in minutes and seconds by a little 'progress bar' showing how much time remains of the song. Everything is called a 'song' now whether it is vocal or purely instrumental, whether it is a song, dance music, an opera or a symphony.

Computer devices for playing music and video seem to think that we need to know how long the whole thing is going to last, and how far through the experience we are. Yet for many people an important element of music is its ability to take us out of a normal consciousness of time. A really good song or piece of music takes us far away from the clock which paces out our mundane activities. As we listen, we dream - at our desk, at our sink or on the train – with no idea whether our mind has been roaming free for a few moments or much more. Music replaces clock time with musical time, a completely other way of guiding our thoughts and feelings through an experience with its own shape, its own build-up of tension and its own resolution. Our favourite songs seem timeless in more ways than one.

How does it alter the experience to be counted neutrally through every second of a favourite song? Lots of people listen to music while seated at their computers. It's hard not to be aware of that little black button relentlessly advancing towards the end of the line. It can produce in your mind a very peculiar clash of conflicting sensations. On the one hand, you travel along the musical road offered by the song, far away from mechanical time. On the other hand, you glance at the 'time remaining' display, and see the end implacably waiting like a brick wall you're about to hit. Sometimes, sinking into a lovely piece of music, you're carried away by its emotion and look up to see that those heartrending final lines are, in fact, not the doorway to a new universe, but merely five seconds from the end. It can be a jarring sensation.

Why do we need to have our music counted out for us in seconds? Would our enjoyment of a dessert be enhanced by a gauge telling us when the last swallow will occur, and the taste finally be gone? Would we be transfixed by the climax of a play if the proscenium arch displayed a progress bar letting us know that the curtain would drop in exactly three minutes? Are there any pleasurable experiences in life which can benefit from this obsessive countdown?

Everyone has got so used to little three- or four-minute chunks of music that long pieces of music seem more and more extraordinary. In the classical field we're increasingly conscious that the works we play are much longer than the things people routinely hear on their iPods. In concerts, we feel we have to warn people of a particularly long piece so that they won't start to feel outraged if the four-minute barrier is breached multiple times. A work of forty or fifty minutes' duration, quite common for us, now seems almost something to apologise for.

Crossing the finish line

I've been reading about the cyclists of Britain's Olympic team, who were so successful in the Beijing Olympics, winning many gold medals. Instead of muddling through in the great British tradition, they approached their preparation systematically with the help of a whole team of experts. They analysed everything from the bikes and tyres to the step-by-step routines of the cyclists and their competitors. They worked in wind tunnels, with frame-by-frame video analysis, with nutritionists and physicists and shoemakers. They were advised on matters of team bonding and positive outlook. With the help of a team psychiatrist, each cyclist was encouraged to identify up to 150 'foundation stones', areas they felt could be worked on to improve their performance and make a gold medal not just a possibility but a likelihood.

It all sounded inspiring and educational, and I was thinking how much I could learn from it – until I stopped to think about how un-transferable it is to the arts world. Just the idea of subjecting any of my own music groups to these methods is laughable – not because we have nothing to learn from them, but because nobody believes that systematic sports methods are applicable to us. Actually, I think we could benefit from such analysis in all sorts of ways peripheral to our music-making: the way rehearsals are run, the way admin is done, attitudes to punctuality, ways of being better prepared for rehearsals, and ways of making travel easier, not to mention the art of team bonding and mutual support. But it is the aspect of measuring which seems so crucial to sportsmen and so beside the point for people in the arts.

At the end of the day, a sportsman must cross the finish line first, jump highest or longest, enter the water straighter, throw the javelin or discus further. These things are all measurable. Whoever does them is the winner, no matter what other qualities of grace or beauty may be demonstrated by other competitors. Steps can be taken to work on this purely measurable goal of getting to the finish line ahead of the others. But the measure of success in the arts world is far less guessable. There are musicians who do indeed play faster, louder, higher than others, but they may make less impact on their audiences than others who are not able to emulate them. As soon as art and emotion come into play, measurement is pointless, which is why ballet is not an Olympic sport, despite the fact that ballet dancers are probably the fittest and strongest of the lot, easily up to Olympic standard. But if ballet dancers were to appear in the Olympic stadium and perform *Swan Lake*, there would be no unanimous judges' marks, no matter how physically fit the dancers were. For in matters of art, where is the finish line? Certainly there are lines that must be crossed for success to register, but the lines vary tremendously and seem to be located in each individual spectator's heart.

August ...

Technique

My bedside reading at the moment is Frances Mayes's charming account of restoring an old house in Cortona, *Under the Tuscan Sun*. She tells of going to a cookery course taught by Simone Beck. One of the class was insistent on trying to get precise measurements of ingredients and descriptions of the culinary techniques being used. Eventually Simone Beck said in irritation, 'There is no technique. There is only the way to do it. Are we going to measure, or are we going to cook?'

In a way this is just playing with words, because 'the way to do it' is just another way of saying 'technique'. But we know what she means, and it is the same with everything that one can do well. Between technique and 'the way to do it', there is a subtle difference.

Measurement is left behind, the recipe is left behind. In a way it is a matter of looking at the end product from completely different angles. The novice looks at the finished dish, performance, or whatever as something they have to approach gradually and step by step. It lies ahead of them on a road they haven't travelled yet. The expert looks at the finished dish as a whole. It lies behind them, so to speak, on a road whose milestones are no longer visible.

*A*rtist unknown

A friend tells me that she's just bought the Beethoven piano trios on CD, so naturally I ask, 'Who's playing them?' 'Oh!' she says. 'No idea. I'm afraid I didn't look at the names of the players.' Why do people seem to think the performer is irrelevant?

A relative of mine recently confessed that although he was becoming quite familiar with the classics of the piano trio repertoire, he doubted whether he would be ever able to discern any difference between performances of those works by different groups. When I express dismay, he says, 'But surely there can't be much difference between top-level musicians playing the same works. Aren't you all aiming at the same result?' By that I suppose he meant that all musicians are trying to arrive at a perfect realisation of that holy text, the musical score. But there's another way of looking at it, one expressed beautifully by musicologist Christopher Small when he pointed out that one might as well turn this perception on its head and consider that it's the job of composers to give musicians something to play. At the end of the day, you can't hear music unless it is played, and it is the character of the playing which most impacts on listeners at the moment of performance. Personally, I wouldn't put the performance *above* the score in order of importance, but I do think the performance is crucial. Well, I would think so, wouldn't I? But as well as knowing that a good piece can be ruined by a bad performance, and that a bad piece can be greatly enhanced by a good performance, I also truly believe that a great perform-ance can bring a good piece to a new level.

I remember hearing Italian soprano Cecilia Bartoli in a programme of rather trivial Italian arias of the baroque and classical periods. Any thought of the music's triviality was however completely driven away by the energy and commit-ment she gave to it, performing it as though she thought it was utterly fascinating. I remember thinking that it was an object lesson in how to perform second-rate music, and in fact I've learned from her example.

But even music of the finest quality can reveal new aspects of itself and even become transcendent in a fabulous perform-ance. Bob still remembers his awe on hearing Carlos Kleiber conduct Verdi's *Otello* at Covent Garden in the 1970s. It's an opera he'd previously heard in fine performances with other singers and other conductors. However, in Kleiber's hands the opera suddenly struck him as a miracle of expressive coher-ence in a wholly unexpected way. Even though he knew the music very well, he was so gripped by the performance that he remained glued to his seat long after the performance had ended, unwilling to break the atmosphere. Later on, he heard that Bernard Haitink had attended the same perform-ance with a fellow conductor and had said to his companion, 'Well, that was the finest evening in the opera house that you or I will ever experience.' Yet what remained for Bob was not the sensation of Kleiber's personality but the conviction that Verdi's *Otello* was even better than he had realised. When he could bear to listen to it again, performed by other people in later years, the effect was not the same. He realised that the alchemy at Covent Garden had been created by music brought to boiling point by particular musicians.

Of course, this kind of experience is not confined to music. How many schoolchildren, bored and irritated by having to study Shakespeare, conclude that there's nothing in it for them until one day they get the opportunity to see a really good performance of one of his plays, when all of a sudden a door is kicked open in their minds.

The piano girls of the south

Bob has been sent a fascinating article by Candace Bailey, about the piano-playing craze amongst young ladies of the American South in the years before the American Civil War (or 'the antebellum years' as the writer puts it). There were so many of them that they were known as 'piano girls'. Piano playing was such a desirable social skill that parents were willing to spend as much money on piano lessons as they did on academic tuition. At boarding schools, the termly bill for accommodation and food was only slightly higher than the bill for piano lessons and for the hire of a piano. This seems stunning today when one considers that piano teachers on an hourly rate are paid far less than garage mechanics or plumbers.

What fascinated me particularly was that although the 'piano girls' of the mid-nineteenth century had access to plenty of music written by middle-European composers, they did not have the works that we consider the backbone of classical piano today, namely the works of Beethoven, Schubert and so on. Their repertoire was squarely based on light music, mainly gentle dances, with particular emphasis on what could be played without exerting yourself physically. Indeed it was sometimes impossible to tackle anything which required athletic movement at the keyboard (such as crossing the hands, or sudden leaps from top to bottom of the keyboard) because of their dresses and the way the sleeves and bodices were constructed. Young ladies were counselled by etiquette books not to attempt to sing or play music which expressed 'a masculine passion'. They were allowed to attempt difficult music in private, but were advised always to restrict their public performances to graceful, easy music. Even the polka was considered a little too flamboyant by many parents.

Though I knew that Beethoven piano sonatas were not played much in public until the end of the nineteenth century, I hadn't realised that Beethoven and Schubert were actually absent from the music libraries of talented young women – at least in America – in the mid-ninteenth century. From studying their 'piano books', collections of sheet music they gradually acquired or copied, it appears that they were not playing Beethoven sonatas even in private. They knew the works of Kuhlau, Heller and Clementi, but not Beethoven. This now seems a kind of Orwellian thought policing. Who was responsible for keeping such music out of their hands? The idea of young ladies playing stormy Romantic music in public must have seemed as distasteful as the idea of watching them climb onto a platform to wrestle with a bear. When did it change? Today, it's the other way round. No talented young pianist can get very far without tackling the works of Beethoven and Schubert, and today's 'piano girls' would think it absurd that men should dictate what they may play.

Janáček's string quartet

It's an exciting moment when the parts arrive for a new piece. Austrian pianist Till Alexander Körber has made an arrangement for piano trio of Janáček's first string quartet, 'Kreutzer Sonata', based on a short story by Tolstoy. Well, it isn't exciting straight away, because the parts arrive in the form of a computer file, from which single pages can be printed out. The sheaf of single pages has to be painstakingly stuck together, a task which takes me most of an evening and uses a whole roll of special book-mending tape. Oh for the day when music can be displayed on a portable electronic screen!

In Tolstoy's short story which inspired the music, Pozdnyshev, disillusioned with marriage, begins to suspect that his wife is having an affair with a violinist whom she meets to play sonatas for piano and violin. Pozdnyshev is jealous of their rapport and plans a *crime passionel*, but when he hears them playing Beethoven's 'Kreutzer Sonata' one day he discovers that the music is powerful enough to change his mood and stay his hand. On a subsequent occasion, he finds his wife at dinner with the violinist, attacks her and kills her. The violinist escapes from the murder scene; Pozdnyshev wants to chase after him, but refrains from doing so because he is still in his socks, and does not want to seem ridiculous by running after his wife's lover in his socks. Later, he travels about on the railway telling his story and seeking forgiveness from fellow passengers.

162

When I was first living in London, after university, I had
a tape of this Janáček quartet played by a wonderful Czech
group, confusingly also named the Janáček Quartet. I used to
play it late at night and became so attached to their performance that I used to play the tape in my car, where I didn't
normally bother to listen to music because the sound quality
was so poor. Anyway, the wildly expressive nature of the
music, and of their performance, transcended the tinny sound
system in my Vauxhall Viva.

I love Janáček's piano music. It's often rather 'ungrateful'
to play, and lies awkwardly under the hand, but somehow
this seems to fit the music. The jerky rhythms and cumula-
tive driving patterns, the blurting-out of melodic fragments,
the relentless chewing-over of jagged little nuggets – all this
makes Janáček's music unique. Obviously I've never had the
chance to play one of the string quartets, so it's exciting to
have an arrangement which involves the piano. I haven't heard
it together with the string parts yet, as our first rehearsal isn't
until the end of next month. Until then I'm just learning the
part on my own.

Janáček did write an early piano trio inspired by Tolstoy's
story, but he destroyed it, so there is no way of knowing
whether the music is the same as that of the string quartet he
composed later. One of my colleagues remarked that there are
lots of passages in the quartet which were probably conceived
at or for the piano, because they lie so awkwardly under the
string player's hand that they can't have been conceived in
terms of strings. But actually they are just as awkward for
me, so perhaps they were not conceived in terms of instruments at all. Beethoven once famously said to a violinist who
complained about the difficulty of one of his violin parts, 'Do
you think the spirit speaks to me in terms of your wretched
instrument?' Janáček is not quite like this – that's to say, not
Olympian – but I can sense that sometimes his music is
designed to stick in the throat of whatever instrument has to
play it. Effort is what he wants to put across, and it's not even
right to try to make it sound frictionless.

Searching for a book whose title and contents I have forgotten

In my local high street there are a number of charity shops, and in between bouts of piano practice I sometimes spend an hour in them for relaxation. A lot of my reading matter is found there. I find it intriguing to see what other people have given away, and would rather come across something unusual in a charity shop than by searching in a bookstore. Having been involved in the clearing out of a couple of older relatives' houses, I now know that there are many reasons for donating things to charity. It does not always mean that the donor was tired of them or thought them worthless, but may simply have had no more store room, or no time to look through the boxes properly before giving them away.

When browsing through the books, I often look through the children's section hoping to find a particular book I loved when I was little. I have never found it, which may be partly because I have forgotten its title and contents. All I really remember is the very particular sensation the book gave me when I was a child. The book was, I think, about animals. It had a grey hardback cover and possibly a country scene on the front, something indescribably delightful. It seemed an old book, though I am not sure where we would have got an old book from. Were there nuts and squirrels? All I remember is that the smell of the book, the weight of it in my hands and the effect of its stories was deeply comforting. It was probably one of the first things I could read for myself. My favourite part of the day was to be told, 'You can go to bed and read now.' I loved to sit up in my cosy bed and read, vaguely aware of my parents pottering about in the adjacent rooms. They were busy, but I was not. Reading was pure pleasure, a reward for having finished my little tasks of the day.

I suppose the book I liked must have been given away, for in later years I could never find it in the house. Some of our books were given or lent to relatives or friends with young children. I've looked in all the likely houses, hoping to find this book again. I can't even ask anyone to look for it, because I've forgotten everything about it except the feeling it gave me. For years now I've looked in antique bookshops and jumble sales and charity shops, holiday cottages, and the book collections of strangers, hoping that by chance I will suddenly stumble upon 'my' book – though whether I would even recognise it I am no longer sure. The title has so thoroughly vanished from my memory that any actual book title might seem wrong. And very likely no other copy of the book would smell exactly the same, its weight in my hands the same as I remember.

Seeming difficulty and its opposite

To make sure there are no slip-ups with my practising, I check the forward schedule of all the pieces I have to play between now and Christmas. Every three months I make a list of pieces for the following three months, and pin it up beside my bedroom mirror so that I can keep track of everything. The list is divided into 'old' pieces on the left hand side, and 'new' on the right. 'Old' means not that they were written long ago, but that I have performed them before.

Unfortunately, it isn't always a straightforward matter to revive 'old' pieces, which sometimes turn out to have developed thorns since I last looked at them. Today, looking at the list, I realise that one of the trio's autumn pieces is the first piano trio by Saint-Saëns. We haven't played it for a few years, and as it turns out, we are playing it only once this autumn, but this still means I have to practise it properly.

When I first learned the piano part, it took me far longer than I anticipated, because it doesn't lie under the hands in the way that other difficult piano music can do. The string parts are simple and elegant, but the piano part is virtuosic. Somehow, Saint-Saëns has contrived dozens of different forms of fast arpeggios and running chromatic passages for which there seems to be no comfortable fingering. I remember that on first learning it I wondered whether I had become stupid. Certainly my hands felt stupid. Over and over, I tried to find fingerings that would easily embed themselves in my mind and become unconscious, a pre-requisite for comfort in performance. Alas, I never found those fingerings and I felt very exposed and unhappy in our performances. My piano part was littered with written fingerings, which is very unusual for me, but I still felt as though I were trying to make my hand conform to shapes which it didn't naturally fit.

Strangely enough, the second piano trio by Saint-Saëns is more achievable even though it is longer, even more technically demanding, and requires considerably more stamina. You can practise it and make progress. Fingerings present themselves quite straightforwardly, and stick in the mind after a bit of practice. Yet in both cases, the trios were written for Saint-Saëns himself to play – one when he was young, the other in later life. Perhaps he had simply learned more about writing for the piano by the time he got to the second trio?

At any rate, going back to look at the first trio once again, I find that once again my hands seem to have gone deaf. They don't appear to hear my mental instructions and keep hitting the wrong notes. I hate to hear myself slowly going over and over passages which will not sink down into the accepting layers of memory. I feel like a beginner again. And most annoyingly of all, I know that the audience will not realise it is difficult, because musically it is straightforward, and is meant to sound simply rippling and luxurious. When I've finished, I go into the kitchen and say to Bob, 'That first Saint-Saëns trio is so unbelievably difficult!' 'Is it?' he says. 'I never realised that from listening to it.'

In many virtuosic piano pieces there's a gratifying match between the difficulty and the audience's correct perception of that difficulty; at least such pieces *seem* hard as well as actually being hard! Then there are pieces which sound difficult, but are what pianists call 'grateful' to play, meaning that the writing fits the hand. With these pieces it's pleasingly possible to have success in performance without killing yourself in the effort. This Saint-Saëns piece is another kind of piano writing, where there is friction between the musical thought and its physical expression.

W*aves and particles*

I'm reading a marvellous book, *Friends and Enemies*' by the psychologist Dorothy Rowe. In the course of explaining how our brains perceive things, she digresses into an explanation of quantum physics (fortunately in clear and simple words) and the different ways that physicists have interpreted the behaviour of subatomic particles. Apparently an electron in some situations behaves like a particle, and in other situations will behave like a wave. 'Einstein argued that quantum particles have definite position and momentum, but these are obscured by wave function.' And some quantum physicists argue that there are situations in which a quantum particle is simultaneously a particle and a wave. This complex interaction, or set of parallel realities, is difficult to measure, and to make things even more elusive it appears that the act of measurement affects the behaviour of what you are trying to measure.

The realm of music may seem to be very far away from all this, but there do seem to be analogies. For any musician who's experienced the effect on them when an audience enters the room, there is nothing surprising in the idea that the addition of an observer changes the behaviour of the thing observed. And even the notion of something which is simultaneously a particle and a wave presents no difficulties to someone who is used to making sense of music. You could say that an individual note is like a particle: musicians know that each note has to be itself, with its own integrity, but at the same time it has to be part of a phrase – or there is no music. A note has to learn its place in the whole line, so that meaning can be created by energy passing along the line – or so that energy can be created by meaning passing along the line. A musician has to be able to hold both particle and wave in his or her mind simultaneously.

A sequence of notes, each 'correct' but unaware of the others, can never produce a line that we understand as music. This is clearly demonstrated by the kind of electronic renditions of musical scores which you can hear everywhere on the internet these days. The individual notes may be in the right place, but as they don't know about one another, there is no intelligent current passing between them, and the musical atmosphere is completely dead. It makes one understand the importance of a living musician.

Exploding ivories

The ivories on my piano keys have become even more fragile lately. Each 'white' piano key has a thin layer of ivory attached to its wooden surface. I have never known the ivories to come off the keys until quite recently, when our weather started having sudden changes of humidity and temperature. A year ago, in a prolonged damp spell, individual ivories started coming loose and falling off, leaving a rough wooden key surface. Even worse, some of the ivories started bowing upwards in a little arch. If I touched those ivories when playing, they would suddenly snap off and fly across the room, often leaving a ragged broken end still stuck to the key. It seemed that the ivories were becoming brittle and unstable. There is no perfect way to mend them. The ones that have simply come off can be stuck back on, but sometimes they don't seem to fit any more. With the broken ones, all I can do is ask Steinway to look out for old piano ivories – though exactly similar ones are hard to come by. Now that ivory hunting has been banned, one can only hope to track down some ivory already in use. If no old ivory can be found, a plastic replacement will be fitted. I feel as if the ivories are gradually deserting their posts.

My piano sits next to an unused open fireplace. We've tried blocking the chimney (when we thought it was too cold), unblocking the chimney (when we thought the room had become too damp), turning the heating on or off, hanging reservoirs of water over the radiator. Nevertheless the spate of exploding ivories continues, and I now have a small pile of broken bits on the side of the keyboard, like a graveyard for tiny elephants.

On a recent concert trip to France I met a specialist piano restorer who was working all through our rehearsals on a very unusual Pleyel Duoclave piano which sat in the same room. The Duoclave is a nineteenth century double-keyboard piano of which there are only something like forty in the world. It's a single extremely heavy instrument, a huge rectangle with a keyboard at either end, like Dr Doolittle's Pushmi-pullyu. A double set of strings were neatly fitted across one another on top of a single soundboard. The idea was to enable piano duets of a particularly homogeneous kind, with none of the usual problems of matching the tone colours and strengths of two different pianos.

I asked the restorer's advice about my exploding ivories. He immediately said I was thinking of it the wrong way round. Ivory does not react to heat and damp, but wood does. The ivory is arching upwards because the wooden key beneath it must be shrinking. The dramatic snapping of the ivories had misled me about the true source of the problem: the wood. This striking diagnosis makes me feel particularly stupid. For a couple of years I have been thinking of the ivory as the volatile material. Now I feel I have been misled by its theatrical behaviour when all along it was the unseen wood that was crying out for help.

On returning from France, I look at the keys in a new way. The restorer's illuminating comments have made me realise that my understanding has been upside-down. It's not the surface, but the unseen base which needs attention. As I play, this thought inspires a peculiar sense of revelation. I feel that the piece I'm playing has a template of 'right notes in the right order' which is mapped invisibly onto the piano. Instead of using my willpower to impose that pattern on the piano as I play, I simply have to become aware of the underlying template located under the keys, and allow my fingers to be drawn to it. Alas, this sensation gradually melts away like a meditation mantra which cannot be held permanently in front of the mind.

September ...

New season's crop

September, and the start of a new concert season. For some reason a musician's working year runs from September to August. Most concert series and societies more or less follow the curve of the academic year, but musicians' summers are often busy as well because music festivals like to cluster around the summer, leaving no natural 'break' for musicians. Holidays have to be taken in the quiet periods which fall where they may.

Looking at this season's schedule gives me a melancholy feeling and a sense of déjà vu. On my shelf, I have diaries going back to about 1980. When I look through any of them, my working pattern seems to have been exactly the same from year to year. On paper, there is nothing but an erratic spread of one-off concerts in a range of places. There has been no career ladder to climb, no hierarchy to conquer. While most of my friends in other professions seem to have progressed from junior to middle to senior to professor, head of department or CEO, and have now even retired or become part-time consultants, the pattern of my year just seems to have repeated itself over and over. Each year I pack my little suitcase, go to the train station or the airport, travel somewhere and play a concert, come home again, and do it again somewhere else another day. I have not become a Senior Pianist, the head of a think-tank on pianism, or the wealthy owner of

175

an international chain of trios which has diversified into its own perfume brand and its own range of evening wear.

If you know something about the musical world, you can spot some kind of progression in the venues mentioned in my diaries. Starting off in the early years with concerts in small British venues (the ones my daughter always referred to by the generic name of Upper Pointlessbury), our schedule now names major cities around the world. Apart from that, however, concert programmes have remained much the same over the years. My repertoire has gradually grown much bigger, but I have been playing great works since the beginning, since those were the ones that drew me into the profession in the first place. So I can't even say I have progressed from playing easy things to playing difficult things, or from safe programmes to adventurous ones; our programmes were imaginative and challenging from the start. Fees have risen slowly over the years, but only modestly, and have hardly changed for some years now. The small audiences for chamber music have always translated into limited budgets, no matter how respected the artists.

This morning there was a report on the radio that barristers working for legal aid projects had threatened to strike if they were not paid more than 'the derisory amount of £91 per hour'. Legal aid barristers work at the thin end of the wedge: 'a commercial barrister earns up to £500 per hour,' we were told by way of comparison. While I was still reeling from this disclosure, a clarification came on the lunchtime news: the £91 per hour was for preparation time only, not for fees paid during the trial itself. *Preparation time!* If I could charge for preparation time, I would have been a multi-millionaire long ago.

After all these years, there is still a sense of fragility which I used to think we would naturally outgrow – or which I thought would mutate into a sense of ease. I now realise that a sense of fragility is endemic to the music profession. If we do not continually 'sell ourselves', and if we don't constantly prove that our standards are still high, the phone will stop ringing and we will discover that younger, cheaper, better-looking or more exotic colleagues have been substituted for us at this or that festival where we used to be favourites. Perhaps there will never be a point where we can sit back and bask in being top of the tree. If I were more of an optimist I could look on this as a positive challenge, for it must mean there is never any danger of becoming stale. But on this cold, misty September morning, the glass seems half empty.

P*icking up cues*

In today's rehearsal with the trio, I again noticed that it is sometimes possible to look away from the others at the start of a piece and yet play the first chord exactly together with them. How is it done? Without knowing it, it must be possible to pick up cues such as breathing, and perhaps noises of bows and strings, which indicate the physical movements of the other players and when they're likely to produce a sound. I sometimes dare myself to look away just to see whether I still have the knack.

Once when making a record with the BBC Singers, conducted by Jane Glover, I had a striking experience of this sort of subliminal cueing. We were recording in a church, St Giles Cripplegate, near the Barbican in London. At the altar end of the church, Jane was facing the BBC singers, and I sat behind the conductor's podium at the grand piano. We were waiting to begin a 'take', but there was some disturbance down at the far end of the church or outside in the street, and we had to wait for the noise to stop. The conductor and choir were on my left, but I had swung away from them onto the side of the piano stool, and was sitting with my back to the conductor, looking towards the noise at the far end of the church. We all waited in silence for the noise to die down.

All of a sudden, my hands flung themselves round to the left (I can't put it any other way) and plonked down on the

178

opening chords of the piece just as the conductor gave the downbeat. Without my being aware of it, Jane had judged it quiet enough to begin, but hadn't thought to look behind her to check that I was also ready. Though I had my back to her and didn't consciously hear or see anything, my hands responded correctly to the cue before 'I' had realised I was needed. My body was still twisting round to face the keyboard as my hands were already playing the opening bar. For a second I had the curious sensation that my ears had migrated to my fingertips.

C major: red, white or blue?

Just before her performance in the Last Night of the Proms, pianist Hélène Grimaud is interviewed on the radio. She speaks about her instinctive ability to see colours when she plays music. We now call this synaesthesia, where listeners can't help 'seeing' certain keys as being particular colours. Hélène mentions that for her, the key of C major is definitely white, but that she does not know whether this conviction is shared by other synaesthetic listeners. She says she imagines it's a personal thing.

So the interviewer invites people to call in with their own definitions of the colours, and during the programme two people do. Both are women. The first says that for her, C major is definitely red, and the other one says that for her, it is definitely blue. So far it looks as if C major is the visual equivalent of the French *tricolore* flag.

For me, C major is probably white, but I am not sure if this is a synaesthetic belief or something a bit more down-to-earth. Hélène Grimaud and I are pianists, and I imagine that the deeply-ingrained sight of the piano keyboard has influenced us to some degree. In C major, a pianist plays only on the white keys, so it makes sense for us to feel that C major is white. However, this doesn't explain why other keys 'are' other colours. Why, for me, is A major red, for example? Why is F major pale blue? Less relevant, but equally interesting: why is Monday red? Why is Wednesday green, and Friday brown?

I would be interested to know whether synaesthesia is only experienced by people with perfect pitch, or more generally. People with perfect pitch have an innate understanding of exactly where on the frequency spectrum are the notes they are listening to. For example, the note A is exactly 'at such-and-such a height'. One could almost point to the note A in the air, locating its perch in an imaginary spatial field. If it is not exactly at that height, it would be another note. Somehow I feel that the relating of keys to colours may be linked to this super-accurate identification of frequency, but don't have enough scientific background to enquire further.

In the middle of the night, lying awake as usual, I ask Bob what colours he links to keys. Sleepily he answers that D is light brown, E major is yellow, F major is green, and then he goes off at an interesting tangent: 'G major has a kind of metallic sheen. A flat major is like velvet,' and so on. He adds, 'It would be interesting to do some research and see whether there is any co-ordination between the light spectrum, the relationships between light frequencies, and the sound spectrum and the relationships between keys.' 'What do you mean by relationship between? Are you talking about mathematical proportions?' But he is already asleep again.

Sunrise over South London

To the Wigmore Hall to play a Sunday morning coffee
concert, always a cheerful thing to do because the audience
is so lively. The BBC is recording the concert and I've been
asked to do a short interview, but as I have a nasty cold I'm
feeling rather self-conscious. To begin with, the sound engi-
neer asks me to say any old thing into the microphone so that
he can adjust the sound levels. So I say what an unusually
beautiful sunrise it was this morning, so radiantly pink that I
went out in the street at 7.30 to watch it until it faded. The
BBC producer says that he was also up at that time, watching
the pink sunrise with his little son. And the sound engi-
neer turns round from the mixing desk and says that he was
watching it too. Somehow the thought of us all watching the
sunrise from our different homes on a quiet Sunday morning
before making our way to the concert hall has dispelled the
tension of the interview, and after that it goes fine.

A couple of years ago I made a Radio 4 programme about
'accompanists' and why many pianists hate that word being
used about them when they play duos with other musicians. We
had set up a series of interviews and we trailed about London
with a tape recorder, asking critics, singers and some well-
known pianists about their experiences of 'accompanying'. I
noticed that although my interviewees were fairly forthcoming
on tape, it was only when the machine was switched off that

182

they really started coming out with anecdotes that would have made the programme's point crystal clear, except that I couldn't use them because they were said in confidence. No matter how casual I tried to be with the set-up, I still felt the interviewee's surge of relief when the tape-recorder clicked off, and an exponential increase in their wish to tell me some really juicy stories about the indignities of being treated as a subordinate. When I later mentioned this to Bob, who has a lot of experience of making radio programmes, he said it was a well-known fact that the 22-carat anecdotes are usually told after you've switched off the recording machine. This gave me a strange sense that what you actually hear on such programmes must be just the tip of the iceberg, with so much material underneath that supports it, but remains inaccessible.

When I think about it, some of my best playing – and that of my colleagues – has arisen spontaneously in rehearsal, where it was heard by only one or two people, or more likely has occurred when practising alone, when it is heard by nobody else at all. Of course you hope that the concert will be the target for your best playing, but that isn't always how inspiration works. In order not to feel too sad about this, one has to hold on to the idea that such moments are not 'wasted', but somehow play a part in giving the world its particular flavour at that moment.

Stravinsky's left hand

Today I was a panellist at an international conference held by CHARM, the Centre for the History and Analysis of Recorded Music. CHARM is coming to the end of a five-year study project and wanted to mark the occasion with a series of special presentations and seminars at Royal Holloway, London University. The centre of Royal Holloway is an enormous Victorian building, on the scale of a palace, with extensive grounds. The music department, however, is not in that central complex. It lies off to the side in a quiet annexe, invisible behind a hedge. As we traipse towards it over the footbridge in the rain, its location feels unpleasantly symbolic.

To counteract the presentations about computer analysis and semantic irregularities, the organisers had decided to invite five performers to share their own experiences of making recordings.

I've always thought that I don't mind my recordings being 'out there' as long as people also have the possibility of hearing me live. Recordings are, after all, partly an artificial construct using the wiles of sound engineers and record producers to shave away our errors and infelicities. I don't regard them as being thoroughly representative of my real playing. There is no doubt that some performers, in pop and classical, use the tricks of the trade to make them sound better than they really are. However, I've more often felt that the danger is the reverse: that the rigour of the recording process slightly dampens the qualities of a really good player, and makes them less engrossing than they are when they perform live.

The conference brought it sharply to my attention that as time goes on, and the performers pass away, the listener naturally loses the opportunity to compare the live playing with the recording. Eventually, the recorded evidence is all they have to go on. From being merely an adjunct of a musician's career, recordings move centre-stage when there are no more live performances, and become the primary source of information. Only the memories of people who heard the players in concert can be set against this information. Now that I see the intensity with which researchers delve into recordings for evidence of what players of the past really did and how they really sounded, I can't help feeling wistful. For my own recordings are by no means my favourite bits of my own playing. They do contain lots of good stuff, but because of the need for accuracy in the recording studio, they probably contain very little of the spur-of-the-moment inspiration which has made some of my concerts so satisfying and fun. Until now I have always felt that that was an annoying but negligible fact. Today in the presence of these musicologists it seems less negligible.

My favourite moment of the day comes in the afternoon when we're discussing the early twentieth century, when composers first had the opportunity to make or supervise recordings of their own music. Bartók, Shostakovich, Webern and Stravinsky are amongst the important composers whose recorded work is now studied in painstaking detail to see if there's any gap between what they said and what they did.

Someone asks conductor John Carewe, one of the panel, for his recollections of Stravinsky. John tells us that as a young conducting student he went to hear every orchestral rehearsal that Stravinsky directed when he visited London in the 1950s. He describes how Stravinsky worked with the orchestra, his severe appearance, how he signalled the character of the bass drum rhythm to the percussionist with big, claw-like movements of his left hand. As he carves the air for us with his own left hand to demonstrate Stravinsky's gesture, John suddenly stops mid-sentence. There's a long pause while he appears to be searching for words, and then tears come into his eyes and he says, 'A bit overwhelming. I'm sorry.' Silence falls on the room as we all wait for him to regain his composure. Nobody moves. '... It's just that ... remembering ...', says John in a choked voice. Suddenly the dry academic atmosphere of the conference is blasted away as everyone realises we are not talking theoretically any more: this is real emotion as one musician remembers the impact of another, working live onstage half a century ago. It's superb.

Tradition

At a meeting today, Jeremy Summerly, a lecturer and director of early music, described the moment he realised he was part of a tradition. As a choral scholar at Oxford University, he sang Evensong in his college chapel every day, working his way through the ancient masterpieces of Palestrina, Byrd and others. The practice of singing Evensong with a specialised choir of men and boys must have been going on in that chapel, and in every similar English chapel, for centuries.

Although he was a choral scholar, however, his personal taste at that time was for modern music. He and like-minded friends spent all their money on the latest recordings and tried to attend the first performances of new contemporary music. One day, he wandered into a friend's room and heard a record of Handel's *Messiah* being played in the version newly recorded by Christopher Hogwood using historical research to get as close as possible to the way Handel might have heard it played. All of a sudden, Jeremy had a Damascene moment, as he described it. The music came alive for him; he realised that he wanted nothing more than to perform it like that, to perform all the music of that period, and then go back and investigate earlier music using similar principles. He suddenly realised that he was part of a long English tradition of sacred choral music. 'Until that moment,' he said, 'I didn't think I was part of a tradition. I thought I was just singing Evensong.'

I relished this remark. 'I thought I was just singing Evensong.' He was like Molière's Monsieur Jourdain, thrilled to discover that, without realising it, he had been speaking prose all his life.

$\mathcal{E}$lie $\mathcal{W}$iesel's voice

While I'm making breakfast this morning, there's a radio interview with the Hungarian Jewish writer and political activist Elie Wiesel, survivor of Auschwitz concentration camp. Wiesel is in London to attend the launch of a Holocaust education programme. He speaks very simply and directly, but what he has to say is memorable. In answer to the interviewer's question, 'Why did you survive when so many did not?', he explains that he has no idea, that he was not specially strong, or brave, and that he was frightened throughout, so scared that he could not look into the faces of the all-powerful camp guards, just as one would not look into the face of God. He makes it clear that he survived not through any effort or intrinsic merit of his own, and he adds that although he has read every book written on the subject of the Holocaust, he is no nearer to understanding the mentality of those who ran the camps. He also says that he is still puzzling over the mentality of the victims. Aggressor and victim are interlocking elements in this never-to-be-resolved conundrum.

In the afternoon, I tell Bob about this interview, and I find that I can remember more or less every word that Wiesel said, including his tone of voice and his accent. However, it seems somehow disrespectful to copy his elderly voice, so I tell it in my own voice. As I do so, it strikes me how much less affecting the speech is when told in my own voice. Without

Wiesel's Jewish accent and the rhythm of his Middle European speech, the text is stripped of identity and seems to be merely information. But I sense that if I had imitated Wiesel's voice, Bob would have been distracted from taking in the content of what he said. How then to convey the haunting quality of the interview? Perhaps Bob, without saying so, will instinctively add an appropriate tone quality to my unadorned words. He will try to imagine Wiesel's voice.

Later on, sitting at the piano, it occurs to me that this problem of 'voice' is one that underlies so much of an interpretative artist's work. If you go to hear a concert and feel that you are hearing only the performer's 'voice' (I don't mean their singing or speaking voice, but their personality), it's never wholly satisfying. All serious musicians try to bring alive the composer's own voice, or at least what they imagine it to be. This doesn't involve pretending to *be* him or her. Nor is it quite a kind of ventriloquism, where you imitate someone else's voice, but try to make it look as if you yourself are not speaking. We all know from experience that there is a way to channel the composer's voice, but how is it done? As the Zen proverb says: 'Do not speak, do not be silent'.

Retreating into music

Driving to the supermarket this morning, I listened to a moving radio feature about a rebel army in Uganda and the suffering caused by their murderous treatment of innocent villagers who got in their way or expressed opposition to them. The Ugandan victims who were interviewed spoke in extremely quiet, hesitant voices. Although they had suffered greatly, they were nevertheless in favour of forgiving the rebel soldiers in order that they could return and be rehabilitated into Ugandan society. Asked whether they could really stomach the thought of such people returning unpunished, the African interviewees quietly answered Yes. They said that there could be no peace otherwise. 'Even though your mother and father were killed by the soldiers?' 'Yes'.

Every so often when I hear this kind of thing I have bouts of feeling that the way I spend my life is completely beside the point. How can it possibly be relevant to spend hours of the day trying to make clear the structure and meaning of a Beethoven piano sonata or a Haydn trio? It feels like an unjustifiable luxury to be concentrating on very refined music which is of interest only to a minority of people. And yet I feel it would be no more helpful or relevant to resign my artistic life in righteous disgust and become an office worker, a librarian or a baker instead. I somehow cling to the feeling that even if what I do has very little practical effect, it

191

must contribute in a small way to the good vibrations in the world. If, as the chaos theorists suggest, the flap of a butterfly's wing might create tiny changes in the atmosphere that may ultimately alter the path of a tornado, then surely pouring beautiful music into the atmosphere may sweep aside harmful vibrations too.

A couple of years ago I was wrestling with similar thoughts during a spate of problems in the Middle East. The *Guardian* had just started its 'Comment is Free' blog, and I was one of a large team of people offered their own page on it. At that time, I was wrestling with Beethoven's A flat major Piano Sonata Opus 110, always a difficult piece to play and to understand. I was hopping from piano to newspaper and from piano to computer, reading about other people's problems in other parts of the world, and the gulf between my preoccupations and theirs was making me feel queasy. I decided to try out the Comment is Free site for the first time with a heartfelt posting. Was I justified, I wrote, in retreating from the political fray into the study of late Beethoven? I ended my post like this: 'I try to work, at and away from the piano, hoping that immersing myself in this great piece will contribute in some mysterious way to a peaceful spirit abroad in the world. Mere fantasy? Head in the sand? Am I one of the passive citizens whose non-engagement is part of the problem? Or am I, in my secular way, following in the long tradition of monks praying for peace, believing that they were creating positive vibrations that would fly out from their monastery walls?'

The reactions, which came seconds after my article 'went live', were quite extreme. They ranged from the hugely supportive to the insulting. 'Susan, you are a wise woman and possibly a saint. I found your post strangely moving', said the very first response. 'Are you a bad person? The answer is yes', snapped someone else. 'Beethoven is not eternal – it just feels that way when you are listening to it', another sneered. 'I'd say you were following in the long tradition of people who live a comfortable lifestyle and don't like to deal with the problems of real people far-away so transfer their fear and guilt (via a whole load of pretentious twaddle) and get overly-vexed about a problem in their own world that is much safer (because it's not really a 'problem') and that probably no-one, other than the author, cares about', wrote another, who was himself immediately shouted down by other contributors for saying so.

Two years later I still feel I need to know what's going on in the world, but I still have no idea whether in the sum of all the human activities taking place at the present moment, it does any good – other than to me – to flap my butterfly wing inside the sanctuary of beautiful music. I believe however that if everyone stopped doing 'insignificant' things, the world wouldn't be a good place to live in.

Farewell to a correspondent

Today I received a letter from the wife of the professor who wrote to me a number of times from hospital about his love of music. He was a very knowledgeable concert-goer and music-lover, though not a player himself. We had never met, but I felt honoured when he wanted to share some very personal insights with me, particularly about late Beethoven and late Shakespeare where his understanding surpassed mine. His wife now writes to tell me that he died yesterday. I am very touched that she should think to include me in the circle of people who need to be told this information. Remembering his hand-written letters and his burning need to communicate his profound responses to music, I realise yet again how mysterious it is that two people who have never met but who know they are both deeply interested in music can dispense with the usual formalities and start talking straight away about things that matter. Out of the blue this man wrote to me, trusting me to understand, and I did.

Contraries

On my 'free day' in Amsterdam, a day between two concerts, I decide to spend the morning practising for an upcoming recital programme. As I'm a visiting artist I'm allowed to practise on the grand piano in the conductor's 'Antechambre', a delightful drawing-room on the first floor, decorated in dove-grey, black and white with a gilded mirror above a white marble fireplace. I imagine that in his time, Mahler must have relaxed here and met with visiting soloists. The key to the room is delightfully labelled 'Antichambre', which sounds like something the sculptor Rachel Whiteread might make, a cast of the space inside a room.

On the wall behind the piano, a proverb is painted in reverse lettering. I squint at it to decipher it. 'All concord's born of contraries', it says in English. Puzzling over why it has been painted backwards, I turn around and my eye falls on the mirror above the fireplace. In the mirror, the proverb appears the right way round. A clever idea, to paint it backwards so that when you gaze into the mirror, you see the contrary. But is it true that all concord's born of contraries? It might be more accurate, though less aphoristic, to add the little caveat, '… if you're lucky'.

P_{lato}

Now and then when performing a work in concert, I manage to play a phrase which strikes me as 'it'. It doesn't happen very often, maybe once or twice a year. What do I mean by 'it'? It's hard to put into words. I don't mean something I've managed to play well, or strongly, or convincingly, or beautifully – hopefully these outcomes occur more than once a year. No, I'm talking of a sense – always fleeting – of playing something like the Platonic ideal of the phrase. How it was in heaven before it was even in the composer's mind, if I could put it like that. It's a sense of going beyond any calculated scheme of expression, beyond the historical context of the music, transcending my own personal thoughts on the matter to coalesce suddenly with a kind of 'original face' of the phrase. It's as though our performances in the real world run parallel with some sort of divine blueprint being played in deep space, outside ourselves. For a split second I feel as if I have seen through the veil.

Is it crazy to speak of 'an ideal' form of something as ethereal as a piece of music? One can perhaps imagine ideal forms, like bowls and plates and jugs, which inventors manage to reach down from their heavenly store and convert into objects we can actually handle and use. Their makers are probably drawing upon some kind of primeval bowl shape which underlies all bowl shapes. But can one say such a thing of a work of music?

196

It seems so at those moments when I turn a phrase, give it a life, when something locks into place for a second or two and I feel, 'That's it!' I don't think it can just be the effect of adrenalin, because that surely would be sustained for longer periods, perhaps throughout the whole performance. If I had a brain scanning device attached, what would it show at such moments? Not much, I suppose, because this doesn't feel like it is the result of brain activity. The sensation of having played 'it' departs almost at once, even if the next phrases are also successfully turned. What is it, then, this brief but vivid sensation of more-than-measurable rightness?

October ...

$\mathcal{D}$ry stone walling

A book lying about in our B&B in Cumbria describes the art of building a dry stone wall. It quotes an old experienced waller as saying, 'One of the rules of dry-stone walling is that you must never pick up a stone and then not use it.' He explains that it's a waste of energy to pick up a stone which you have to put down again. This strikes me as a mysteriously Zen-like statement.

When I start to think about it, I realise that he's expressing the thought obliquely, maybe on purpose. Of course there's no point in picking up a stone and then insisting on putting it into the wall whether it's the right stone or not, simply to avoid the exertion of putting it down again. No, the point must be to not to pick up a stone until you see the right stone to pick up. And that is where the art lies! Yes, it is a waste of energy to pick up any other stone than the one you need next. But we do indeed waste lots of energy in this way. When I think of all the times I have metaphorically bent down and picked up heavy stones I had to put down again, or which I put into my wall against my better judgement …!

In praise of idleness

My local charity shop, usually my source of books to take on concert trips, has come up with Bertrand Russell writing 'in praise of idleness' in 1932. Bertrand Russell is what's nowadays called an iconic figure for me. Coming across the three volumes of his autobiography in my school library as a teenager was a breakthrough moment for reasons which would probably sound strange if I put them into words. However, it was to do with the realisation that there were people out there, people like him, who exchanged ideas and experiences as if it were truly important to know one another's minds. Like many British people, I came from a background where talk was mainly of practical matters. To talk of feelings and ideas was considered to be showing-off, and, probably, causing trouble, 'drawing attention to yourself'. Therefore Russell's letters to and from his intellectual friends came as something of a bombshell. Decades later I can still quote some of the passages which as a teenager I read with such gratitude that they were seared into my memory.

'In praise of idleness' is not one of his daunting essays, but a plea for more leisure. He points out that many of the achievements of civilisation have been dreamed up, thought out, invented by people at leisure. He thinks it ridiculous that some people (like himself I suppose) have inherited leisure, while others have no choice but to work long hours. We all need more leisure, he thinks.

Is playing music 'work'? For amateurs it has always been considered leisure, but in the past hundred years, and especially in the last few decades, being a professional musician has become more and more definitely work. Because of the demands of international travel combined with the modern audience's CD-trained expectation of technical perfection, 'keeping one's playing up' has become a treadmill. Today's professional musician knows that concert promoters and agents look up all their reviews on the internet. If they have an off-day in Tokyo or Paris, the fact is not easy to disguise. And as expectations have grown, the sheer amount of time spent playing the instrument – in private practice, rehearsal and concert – has grown too. A performing career is now punctuated by anguished visits to the physiotherapist and to other kinds of therapist.

I have a friend who runs a very good orchestra for school-age musicians. Most of the members want to be professional musicians, but even those who don't have already gained high marks in their Grade Eight exams and diplomas. They're excited about music, and their aspirations are high, especially when they've spent time together and heard about one another's achievements. They meet in the holidays and play a concert at the end of the week. At the last meeting, my friend told me that several players had had to drop out during the rehearsal period because of physical aches and pains. She had had to drive at least one of them straight to a chiropractor for emergency treatment. When I went to listen to their final rehearsal, another member of the orchestra was listening at the side of the room because her arms were too painful to join in. Two members of the orchestra were quietly dropping their violins to their laps at various points during the play-through, because recent bouts of tendonitis did not allow them to tackle the whole programme at a single stretch. It struck me as extraordinary that these young people, still fledglings in the profession, should already be suffering physical burn-out.

Against this background it was good to be reminded by Bertrand Russell that there are other ways of making progress. In fact, we're crazy if we overlook the mind's capacity to digest information while off the boil. Many thinkers have had their best ideas when sitting under apple trees, staring out of a train window, dreaming during a daytime nap, etc. Just this week we heard that Professor Peter Higgs, after whom the so-called Higgs Boson – the 'god particle' which the new Large Hadron Collider at CERN in Switzerland is searching for – is named, had dreamed up or sensed its existence while walking in the snow one Christmas holiday. Of course all these people had to prepare the ground by doing the work first. But we should notice that the breakthrough ideas did not come when they were at their desks or in the laboratory.

$\mathcal{I}_n$ *reverse order*

These days, the Wigmore Hall in London (or 'Wigmore Hall' as we're now supposed to call it, the definite article having been stylishly dropped) is my favourite hall, but the first time I played there was not a thoroughly happy experience.

When I was eleven years old my piano teacher in Edinburgh, Miss Mary Moore (whose title had definitely not been dropped), entered me for the National Junior Piano-Playing Competition. It started with regional heats, and I won the Scottish heat, so I was invited to come to London for the finals, which took place in the Wigmore Hall. This meant months of preparation, a new red dress made by my mother, and a 400-mile trip to London with her on the train. It was all so momentous that I felt sick on the train. We stayed in the YMCA in Great Russell Street, where I solemnly recorded the canteen dishes of the day in my orange Baberton spiral note-book ('grapefruit followed by lamb with macedoine vegetables and two kinds of potatoes, sliced and roasted, with gravy. Ice cream for me, greengages for Mummy'). I seem to remember that there was an upright piano somewhere in the YMCA and that I was allowed to practise on it.

I suppose that competitions haven't changed much over the years; in any case, I remember the stiff atmosphere between us young competitors and our various entourages of families and piano teachers, the teachers out-psyching one another with pre-performance routines designed to give their own students an edge and make the others feel less secure. I think Miss Moore (who had also travelled down from Scotland) advised me not to listen to the other competitors, so all I remember are fragments of my own time on stage, especially the playing of a slow Schumann Romance in F sharp major which I felt was particularly 'mine' and which was kindly praised by one of the judges, Phyllis Sellick, who said it was her favourite moment of the evening. I felt wonderful in my red Viyella dress with a tiny white lace border around the neck and sleeves, and a sticking-out skirt.

After the last competitor had played, we finalists milled nervously about backstage while our supporters sat with the general public in the hall, waiting for the judges to make their decision. A smiling official stepped into the Green Room and, touching me gently on the arm in front of this keyed-up throng, propelled me gently over to the door that led directly to the stage. Everyone watched this intently, whispering among themselves. Without speaking, she then went over to Neil Wilson and led him over to stand behind me, and finally she brought over Jonathan Dunsby, who stood third in line. So I must have won! Smiling encouragingly but wordlessly, she stood by the three of us until we heard a burst of applause from inside the auditorium. The door to the stage was flung open from the far side, and she gently pushed me on stage. I emerged into the stage lights to find everyone clapping and beaming at me. I bowed, shook the judges' hands, and stood to the side as they indicated. Then on came Neil Wilson to another burst of clapping. I dimly heard them say, '... who receives the second prize.' And then to yet more enthusiastic clapping, on came the other boy and I heard them say, 'Ladies and gentlemen, the winner of the National Junior Piano Playing Competition, Jonathan Dunsby.'

'The winner' ...! So what was I, then? Trying to hold the smile steady on my face, it dawned on me that if Jonathan was the winner, and Neil had won the second prize, I must have won the third, although I had not heard anybody say so. I had not yet encountered the tradition of announcing the prize winners in reverse order, and nobody had thought to warn me that such a thing might happen. Everyone started surging around Jonathan to congratulate him and take his photograph. I remember standing there, ignored by everyone and trying not to cry as my imagined triumph evaporated. I recall that moment every time I see the runner-up at the Wimbledon Tennis Championships during the prize ceremony – sitting quietly on the margins while the winner enjoys his or her moment of glory.

Much later, back home again, I was persuaded by my teacher that winning third prize in a national competition at age eleven was a fine thing to have done anyway, 'especially for a girl'. But the experience marked my feelings about the Wigmore Hall for years and years, and when I am on stage there these days, I sometimes imagine my childish self standing bewildered to one side. I still think it's a good example of how competitions can undermine the confidence of young players.

Winning a big competition doesn't always lead to happiness, of course. When I re-entered the competition a couple of years later, the overall winner was the ten-year-old Terence Judd. Terence, an outstanding talent who embarked very early on a glittering solo career, committed suicide by jumping off Beachy Head at the age of twenty-two.

Everything in my shop is the best

Zen Flesh, Zen Bones, a delightful collection of Zen anecdotes, tells a story which means a lot to me.

> 'When Banzan was walking through a market he overheard a conversation between a butcher and his customer.
> 'Give me the best piece of meat you have', said the customer.
> 'Everything in my shop is the best', replied the butcher. 'You cannot have any piece of meat that is not the best'. At these words Banzan became enlightened.'

I often think of this tale when comparing the attitudes of people who try to play their best all the time with those who strategically play their best only when they think there are witnesses. Some very fine players 'save themselves' for the concert, as though other music-making is less meaningful. The outstanding musician and violinist Gidon Kremer was like this when I attended his festival in Austria. In rehearsals he would often do what opera singers call 'marking' when they want to save their voices: not really playing, but just sketching in the violin line, often with his violin held casually against his chest. Those who played chamber music with him could only check timing and co-ordination, but could not gauge how full his violin tone would be in the concert, or what colours. He liked to save his energy for the performance, when he depended on his colleague's quick thinking to adjust to the full dimensions of his sound. This came as a surprise to me, and I suppose it arose because he had programmed himself into so many pieces during the festival, with the result that he was on the go day and night, and had to conserve his resources. However, I would never dare only to sketch in the piano part like that in rehearsals, as it deprives everyone else of so much essential information. It seems to me a matter of courtesy to play in rehearsal with the same tonal spectrum one intends to use in the concert. I never, or almost never, knowingly underplay. The 'almost' allows for some of those really heavy modern grand pianos I encounter now and then in concert halls, and whose action is so challenging that I sometimes have to go easy on myself in rehearsal in order to save my muscles, particularly if the rehearsal is immediately before the performance.

My ambition is to be like the butcher in whose shop every piece of meat is the best – whether anyone comes in to buy it or not. However, setting oneself this goal doesn't always have the results one might hope for. Was it the composer-pianist Busoni who advised that every so often one should deliberately throw in a wrong note or a split octave just to remind people that playing the piano is difficult? People who manage to achieve consistency are so often taken for granted, and sometimes it feels as if the opposite strategy would be more effective.

$\mathcal{E}$xplanatory labels

Bach's *St John Passion* comes on the radio while I'm eating toast. Someone is singing the beautiful aria 'Es ist vollbracht', with which Christ acknowledges that 'it is fulfilled'. Bob points out that the theme of the aria is the same as Beethoven's slow movement theme in his Piano Sonata in A flat, Opus 110. I have never known this in all the years I've studied and performed this work, nor has any teacher mentioned it. Beethoven heads the slow movement 'Klagende Lied' (song of complaint, or lament) and must consciously have been quoting Bach. This is an important historical link between the two works, and gives depth to the later one.

However, although I'm ashamed not to have realised the link before, the discovery doesn't really illuminate anything that wasn't already clear in the Beethoven. The way he arrives at his lament, the context, the exhausted rhythms he invents to underlie it, the way the theme develops, fragments, sinks back – all make the meaning perfectly clear. It's both intellectually satisfying, and touching, to know that Beethoven quotes Bach at this extreme moment, but it doesn't unlock anything that was hidden. This I think is a tribute to Beethoven. How many times in art is meaning conferred on a new work by a conscious invocation of something else which the artist uses to make his new work seem more resonant than it actually is? So many, many times in art galleries or exhibitions have

I looked at a work without getting much from it, and then stepped forward to read the printed explanation by its side, only to find that the work is supposed to 'reference' something or other which I would never have guessed. I came across a very good example when visiting Mozart's birth house in Salzburg. In its little museum was a room hung with framed engravings of Salzburg churches – but every picture was hung upside-down. At first it looked like a ludicrous mistake. Then I read the 'explanation' that the inverted pictures represented Mozart's playful habit of looking at things in a new way. To me this kind of thing is no more than a lazy pretence at meaning. The viewer is invited to superimpose the explanation on the 'artwork', which cloaks itself in qualities borrowed from something more powerful.

Beethoven is not like this. His invocation of Bach adds another layer to a narrative which he has already made perfectly clear, and which already has a moving and spiritual atmosphere without needing to remind the listener of the link to an older religious work. This seems to me an important difference between the type of artist who has to tell you what the meaning is, and an artist who doesn't even bother to mention the 'reference' because the meaning needs no external support.

*P*urring along

Performing Mendelssohn's Variations Sérieuses in public for the first time, I step back enough to enjoy just playing the piece without monitoring my own progress in an inhibiting way. Often, when I'm worried about whether I'll be able to play something successfully in public, I follow my own hands as I play with a coldly judgemental eye, or worse: with a kind of out-of-body sceptical observation which paradoxically makes it much more likely that I will make mistakes. Tonight, however, I manage to keep that particular cage door shut in my mind. The Mendelssohn purrs along, with me as the relaxed driver. Afterwards, my friend Margaret says, 'That Mendelssohn has obviously been in your fingers for a long time!' Hard to remember that only a few weeks ago I was despairing of ever reaching performance standard.

Every performer must know the strangely detached feeling of watching themselves play, waiting for themselves to come off the rails. Yet who wants you to come off the rails? Not the audience. Why then? There's an inherent schizophrenia which many players can only combat by making sure they know the piece inside and out before they have to walk on stage and perform it. They need to know that other physical systems will have their own chance of carrying the performance along successfully despite the interference of the little demon voice, the little doubting eye which watches the hands untrustfully. As usual, the underlying task is one of trying to unite the inner and outer selves.

Annoyingly, this monitoring self, the one who prods and analyses, is necessary all the way along the learning path until the moment when it becomes a handicap. But how can one practise turning it off? You can't know how it will affect you in performance until the moment of performance, when it's too late to practise hearing yourself innocently and without disapproval.

Recession

The newspapers are full of dark predictions of recession and unemployment. I have never known such a sudden economic crisis, which appears largely to be the fault of bankers and their 'financial instruments' such as selling packages of debt to other banks and financial institutions. Overnight we laymen have all become experts on the sub-prime mortgage crisis in America, of which we had never heard a month ago. Everyone predicts a return to basics, a cutting down on luxuries, tightening of belts. Only a moment ago we were hearing nothing but dazzling stories of celebrity lifestyles, sky-high bonuses and thousand-dollar lunches, but suddenly it seems to be over. Now they are talking about people losing their jobs. Many projects will have their funding slashed. At such a time I waver wildly between being sorry that I am a musician, and glad. Part of me wishes I had a useful, sensible job through which I could play a part in restoring things to order. Part of me is happy to be engaged in something which has enduring value independent of things like money markets. Will people want music more, or will it become increasingly irrelevant? Already in the past week several people have said to me things along the lines of, 'Thank goodness for music, where we can remind ourselves about what really matters!' But of course it does not 'really matter' in any practical way. It is certainly not an item on everyone's shopping list. Life may well be about to get even harder for musicians, though it's also possible that live music may mean more to those who still make the effort to come and hear it.

Bob says there is no point in my giving up music in order to do a useful job. So many people can do things better than I could, but Bob says there are not so many who could take my place in the music scene. He says that if you can do something really well, you should do it, because it's contributing something particular to the world which might not otherwise be contributed. In any case, I am not trained to do anything else, though I quite often fantasise about re-training. I have never been sure whether I'm of more use to my community as a pianist or as, say, another teacher or nurse or local councillor. Whenever I'm feeling most doubtful about music, something happens to restore my faith, such as the letters I received after last Saturday's solo recital. 'We would travel anywhere to hear you', and so on. Clearly there is something valuable to be given.

I always remember my friend Gerald, faced with the choice between being a singer and being a lawyer: 'I didn't mind the thought of being a second-rate lawyer, but I was damned if I was going to become a second-rate musician.' This has always been my favourite story about Gerald. In fact, he had the best of both worlds: he became a first-rate international lawyer, and was able to keep singing as a hobby which still delights him in his seventies.

Cathedral Cave

Visiting the Lake District for a few days of walking with Bob and his brother Anthony, we fall into conversation with a couple on the same walk. They ask us if we've ever seen Cathedral Cave, an abandoned quarry quite close by, a remarkable sight but one not advertised in the leaflets about walks because of its dangerous condition. They show us the entry, up the hill and through a tunnel dripping with water. At the far end, we emerge into a vast cave quarried out beneath the hillside, one huge pillar of rock still left to prop up the ceiling. Far above our heads, light breaks through a collapsed rock wall. The echoing space inspires us to try out our voices. What do we sing? I find myself singing, 'O God make speed to save us', the chant I heard at Evensong recently in the chapel of King's College Cambridge. The huge dark cavern is completely secular in purpose, yet it seems right to sing something devotional. Bob, Anthony and I sing three-part chords, which expand and bloom like lilies, luminous in the stone-cold twilight. The people who brought us in are amazed. 'Where did you learn to do that?'

The cave is a strangely compelling place and reminds me of the underground church in St Emilion, likewise dug out of the rock, though with a very different purpose. We stand there in silence for a while listening to the drip-drip-drip from the walls. From far away, I hear childish singing which at first

I think I'm just imagining. It gets louder until eventually a party of schoolchildren, all wearing bright red rock-climbing helmets, emerges into the cave from an unknown tunnel at the far side. They have been exploring the cave system under the mountain. Led by their teacher, they advance gaily into the light like a cheering reversal of the Pied Piper story.

November ...

Lecture recital

To Antwerp, where the music projects organiser has asked the trio to try out a new type of pre-concert talk. They often hold such events, but generally it is a simple lecture by one person talking about the music the audience is going to hear that evening. Today, the organisers want to have me and my colleagues on stage during the talk, chipping in with our own observations (in English) and illustrating parts of the music by playing them. They've cleverly seated the audience on the stage with us for this talk.

Clearly the idea appeals to the concert-goers, because a large number of them come to the lecture recital, many more than usually attend the pre-concert talks. Tonight's topic, the piano trio by Ravel (which we're going to play in the evening concert) is a particularly hard nut to crack. But as we talk, playing excerpts, describing how we feel about them or why they're effective, I see faces begin to light up in the audience – not wholesale, but pinpoints of enlightenment here and there as people 'get it'. In particular I'm pleased that some of the happiest smiles are on the younger faces in the audience – students in their twenties.

It's rather sweet when the presenter asks us why Ravel's piece is simply called 'Trio'.

For a moment I can't think what she means. Does she mean that it lacks a programmatic title, such as 'Sad Birds' or

'Pavane for a dead Infanta'? My mind races, wondering what name Ravel could have given this particular piece. Grand visions of titles like 'From Heaven to Hell and Back', or 'The forest of interlocking paths' suddenly suggest themselves. But it turns out that she only wonders why he didn't call it 'Trio in A minor'. The austere titles of classical music such as 'Symphony' or 'Concerto' or 'Quartet', once considered dignified, now often seem so blank and secretive in comparison to the colourful, imaginative, often deliberately bizarre names which pop and rock groups give to their music.

One of the drawbacks about pre-concert talks like this, and a reason we don't offer to do more of them, is that it's tiring and distracting to talk about the music for a full hour just before our own performance. You might think that analysing it would focus your mind even more on the music, but curiously it often has the effect of making you feel slightly at arm's length from it. It can make you feel as if the subsequent concert is not the thing itself, but the illustration to a lecture being silently given alongside. The music should be the primary experience, but because words are so much more easily understood, they can seem to be the dominant material, with the music playing second fiddle. Pointing things out to the audience, even if they are true things, can lead to a fatal sense of being at one remove from where we as musicians need to be, in the midst of it all.

The British Grenadiers

I'm in Edinburgh to visit my father in hospital. He's very tired and depressed, speaking only in brief phrases. His temperature has made him hallucinate. He is not sure what day it is, what time of day, who has been to see him, whether he has eaten or not. He doesn't feel like opening his eyes or answering any questions. In low spirits I sit by the bed, racking my brain for snippets of information that might cheer him up. My only success so far has been an anecdote about my sister's new kitten, who this morning was sitting on the shelf by the computer monitor, watching the letters appear as I type and trying to pluck them delicately off the screen with his paw. This actually made my father smile, though he didn't open his eyes or say anything.

Suddenly he pipes up with a whole verse of 'The British Grenadiers', a version they used to sing in the Fleet Air Arm during World War II, complete with all the names of the aircraft they used to fly, the whole thing sung perfectly in rhythm and in tune. In the stunned silence of the acute surgical ward this has an extraordinary effect. Ordinary speech has been so difficult for him, and yet here was a burst of music with all the words intact, the tide of music carrying along a cargo of vocabulary which is otherwise lost or inaccessible. If I had said to my father, 'Can you remember the names of the planes you flew in 1943?' I feel sure he would have shaken his head mutely. Yet the whole list comes effortlessly with a tune to carry it. My sister, a psychologist, says it is because when words and music are combined, the two halves of the brain have to work together.

Chopin Waltzes

While waiting for visiting hour at the hospital, I discover a volume of Chopin Waltzes on my sister's piano and spend half a morning playing through them.

They're wonderful music, full of graceful arabesques and sweeping curves, all of them suggesting a certain freedom of rhythm. To play them strictly in time would be ludicrous, a straitjacket which Chopin had clearly cast off with joy. It reminds me of a conversation with someone who had heard both Billy Mayerl and Caryl Gibbons playing live piano music for the tea dances at the Savoy Hotel in London in the 1920s and 30s. Billy Mayerl was the better pianist, said my friend, but he didn't keep strict time, sometimes allowing himself leeway if he wanted to linger over something, sometimes taking off like a rocket if he felt like playing one of his pieces at top speed. Caryl Gibbons, on the other hand, kept his tempos steady and was considered the better pianist for dancing.

These days one doesn't often get the chance of hearing live piano music played for ballroom dancing, but I was lucky enough to hear it at Schloss Elmau in Bavaria before it was renovated and the style of entertainment modernised. They used to have wonderful balls based around the Quadrille, a dance familiar to me only from its appearance in Lewis Carroll's poem about lobsters, whitings and snails. People used to travel from all over Germany for the Quadrille, which

224

was complicated enough to merit its own special instruction session in the afternoon. It was a little like a formal Scottish country dance, danced in groups of four couples each, only with more languorous music. In the evening, the participants would reappear in their finery, the ladies with long 'sticking-out skirts' of heavy, swirly fabric and dancing pumps with little heels and a strap across the instep, buttoning at the side. Watching their dreamy faces, it was clear they felt transported back into the nineteenth century, as I did too.

A pianist played beautiful nineteenth-century dance music on a little stage at one end of the room, her vantage point allowing her to watch the dancers and make adjustments accordingly. Each quadrille lasted about a quarter of an hour because of the many set patterns and sections involved. Dancers would sometimes get in a muddle, especially if children were involved. If this happened, the pianist was able to hesitate or to pause between little sections of the music to accommodate them.

My favourite moments were at the end of swirling sections, when the pianist paused subtly to allow the ladies to twirl to a close, their skirts continuing to swish gracefully for a second after the wearer had stopped moving. It all seemed delightfully dovetailed, making full use of the live pianist's ability to respond to what was actually happening on the dance floor. And of course it worked the other way round, as well: if the pianist played a little faster, the dancers stepped a little faster too. If she paused to turn the page, they took a breather. How warm and human it seemed when set beside modern ideas of music to dance to.

A *special sort of identification*

I hate having nothing to read on the bus, so when going to visit my father in hospital I grab a copy of *Readers' Digest* which is lying around. In the November issue there's an article by the author Alexander McCall Smith about an amateur orchestra he founded in Edinburgh, the Really Terrible Orchestra. He plays the bassoon terribly in it, or so he says, but he has a lot of fun. He writes, 'Members of our orchestra have been astonished at how even our bad and sometimes discordant playing can give pleasure to our audiences. This may be because the listener knows that the music is being made by somebody just like him or her and perhaps this allows for a special sort of identification.'

That same evening, I attend a school concert in which my nephew is playing. There are several orchestras and bands involved, with different age ranges and standards. It's an impressive community effort choreographed with precision, determination and the wholehearted participation of several music teachers who turn their hands to conducting, singing, arranging, playing percussion instruments and guitars as required. The atmosphere in the hall is very supportive: we all know what lies behind the participation of these children who could so easily be wasting time on much less benign pursuits, and we're glad they're here, playing Vivaldi and 'In the Mood'.

Suddenly, the stage curtains part to reveal the school's award-winning pipe band, an ensemble of fifteen kilted pipers and ten kilted drummers all in full Highland dress. Led by a formidably stern pipe major, they burst into an electrifying medley of Scots tunes with resonant historical titles such as 'The 8th Argylls Crossing the River Po'. Around the melodies, the drummers weave an intricate, superbly unanimous web of decorative rhythms. It's by far the most artistically accomplished performance of the evening, and for me the most uplifting, yet I notice that the applause has a certain muted quality to it, as though the very perfection of the ensemble has chilled the hearts of the mums and dads, who secretly prefer the stumbling efforts of the junior training band. The precision piping and drumming is a touch intimidating, and not nearly as endearing as the sight of the three little brass players who hang back in the wings too long to get to their own chairs in time for the concert band pieces, and who sit humbly at the edge of the band without their music stands or music, not playing a note during the performance, and trying to make themselves invisible to an audience who has eyes only for them.

Yes we can

Got up in the middle of the night and turned on the television to see how the American presidential election was going. At 5am I was able to see Barack Obama give his victory speech live from Grant Park in Chicago. There was hardly a dry eye in the audience, and I felt emotional too. As one of the commentators said, by electing a black African–American as President, America had firmly slammed the door on its racist past forever. Like many others, I didn't really think I would see this happen. I just know it's one of those 'Do you remember where you were when …?' moments.

My daughter has been studying the speeches of ancient Greek and Latin orators at university, and of course we have often wondered what they really sounded like, how the respected art of Rhetoric was actually put into practice. Listening to Obama speak, one could imagine that he is a living example. Quite apart from what he says, the intonation of his speeches is a pleasure. He seems to have a natural mastery of the art of phrasing, the intelligent use of breathing and pauses, the melodic rise and fall, and an instinctive understanding of where the cadences of his sentences and paragraphs are. I don't mean that his presentation is manipulative – though it *is* effective – but that he seems to feel naturally how to harness content and delivery.

When these two things are divorced, the speech melody

betrays it straight away. The dull, flat intonation of George W. Bush, for example, always sounded as though he was not mentally engaged with the content of what he was saying, and the gabbled rhythm of his spoken words was often too fast for the meaning, like someone reading a script in a language they don't completely understand. Obama's sense of speech rhythms is gripping. Of course, the main and crucial attribute of his speeches is that *he has something to say*. No doubt he does also have speechwriters, but it is perfectly clear that his ideas and convictions are his own. It may sound simplistic, but I've often noticed that when someone genuinely has something to say, in whatever walk of life, the power of that desire makes them compelling speakers, no matter what their style.

In Obama's acceptance speech he often used the phrase 'Yes we can', one of his campaign slogans, and the way he used the little phrase to punctuate the speech was fascinating, a kind of recurring bass beat in the overall aria. This musical way of speaking didn't distract from the content, but enhanced it, making his words stick in the mind much more effortlessly than with many politicians. Somehow one felt the echoes of much older ways of speaking to crowds, a freedom to range up and down the register of vocal melody, as though he was treading lightly on the border between speech and singing.

$\mathscr{W}here\ is\ art?$

I find it rather scary that when I'm sitting in the hospital ward, just as a visitor, I start to feel that the art (music or words) which occupies my head for so much of the time is starting to ebb away. I become gradually attuned to the quiet and simple atmosphere in which the patients live, just waiting for time to do its work, whether that is in the direction of healing, or the opposite. From time to time my father, or someone else in the ward, asks for help with something or other and I have become very aware of how unskilled I am, or at least how unused I am to helping other adults with very basic needs. I admire the nurses, who seem to take it so much in their stride when someone needs help with going to the loo, turning over in bed, having a blanket bath, needing a change of pyjamas or help with feeding themselves. At such times I am shooed out to wait outside the discreetly drawn curtains, and I earnestly wish that I had the nurses' physical ease and competence at dealing with ill people, instead of feeling the semi-squeamish delicacy and shyness of the outsider. Emerging from the curtains, the nurses give me a brisk smile as though they know very well my city manners are no help at a time like this.

Inside my head, it is rather silent as I sit and wait for the next thing to happen, the arrival of the tea trolley or the next dose of medicine. Instead of being able to sustain myself with inwardly played symphonies or favourite Broadway melodies,

I find that music of any kind seems a little remote. Not just music, but art or literature, which I sometimes bring with me in the form of magazines and novels, or even blank pieces of paper on which I planned to write something. All of it seems like overheated bleating from a parallel universe. Here, the matters uppermost in everyone's mind are: am I in pain, am I warm, am I safe? Is it quiet, am I thirsty, is there someone to hear me when I speak? These questions expand to fill the quietness of the ward and seem to crowd out any thoughts of art, poetry and sophistication. Not only am I aware of the patients thinking this way; I start to think this way myself, and after a short while can hardly imagine any other mental agenda. It's disconcerting that art seems to fade so quickly, and it remains out of my grasp on the journey home as well, only starting to whisper intriguing thoughts to me when I'm back among people who are active and well.

$\mathcal{G}eese$

My sisters and I are discussing our father's illness. We wonder whether we can hope to see him return to his old self, making puns and jokes, mowing the lawn in his suit, offering everyone Battenberg cake or Swiss Roll along with his beloved pots of tea, making a terrible face if his own cup isn't sweetened with three spoonfuls of sugar. Will he go back to waiting for us on his doorstep a quarter of an hour before we're due to arrive? If it's evening, will he still ask us if we've switched on our electric blankets?

My sister's house is on the top of a hill overlooking Edinburgh, with a huge panorama from the living-room window. We sometimes just sit watching dusk fall, as we're doing now, because the changing colours are so dramatic seen from this vantage point. Suddenly my sister says, 'Look!' A huge flock of geese is flying high over the city, spread out in their V formation. The setting sun outlines them in gold like an old illustration from a Hans Andersen fairy tale. Oblivious of us, they plough sturdily onwards into the darkening sky.

A voice from the past

An old college friend, the tenor John Graham-Hall, has asked if I'd be interested to learn Schubert's *Winterreise* song cycle with him. Mark Padmore recently referred to *Winterreise* as the 'King Lear' of song cycles. It's ages since I worked seriously with any singers on Lieder, a repertoire I love. I would like to play more Lieder, but in recent years I've steered myself away from working with singers, because there are so few whose egos don't overbalance the whole musical interchange.

Johnny and I are due to meet in a few days time to try out some of the songs and see how it feels. In preparation for this, I've been looking at the piano part of the Schubert songs, and also listening to a number of recordings. Bob wrote a brilliant chapter on *Winterreise* for an Open University course recently, and I've been listening to the recordings with his book to hand. One afternoon, having listened to the whole of Bob's favourite recording by Peter Schreier and Andras Schiff, we move on to listening to historical recordings made as far back as the 1930s.

We have an ex-au pair from Germany staying with us this week. She and her husband return from a visit to Madame Tussaud's just as Bob and I are listening to Georg Henschel singing on a 1930s recording. On hearing this recording, our German friends shudder and exchange gloomy looks. 'Third Reich', says one to the other. 'What do you mean?' we ask. They explain that Henschel's way of enunciating certain vowels and consonants is redolent of the way that the high-ranking Nazis spoke. Which is not to imply that Henschel himself had anything to do with the Nazis, but that his way of speaking evokes a certain era. 'Which vowels and consonants?' They try to explain the subtle differences between the way certain words are pronounced today and the way they were pronounced by the ruling party in the 1930s, but to my English ears the difference is extremely slight, certainly too slight to provoke the feeling of unease my German visitors feel on listening to it.

I pride myself on being sensitive to nuances in sound quality, but clearly there are areas of language where natives of a country will be extremely alert to styles of speech and their historical associations, resonances to which an outsider is deaf because ignorant of the context. For me, Henschel's singing just sounds like clearly articulated German of a slightly pedantic kind, but I can't hear any sinister overtones. By way of coda to this experience, my guests say how surprised they were to see at Madame Tussaud's a waxwork model of Hitler, surrounded by laughing tourists taking photos of themselves with him. 'That would never happen in Germany.'

Empty steps

On a stormy, blustery night we venture out to see the Mark Morris Dance Group give the London premiere of *Romeo and Juliet* at the Barbican. An American musicologist has unearthed a copy of Prokofiev's uncut score, twenty minutes longer than the one we know, and with a happy ending to the story. This offers a rare chance to hear some Prokofiev music we've never heard before, along with the pleasure of seeing what the brilliant Mark Morris has choreographed for it.

A couple of years ago, a Mark Morris programme at Sadlers Wells was my favourite dance evening ever. So often, particularly with classical ballet, I feel a sense of frustration that the dancers' steps are not actually to the music, but merely run in parallel with it. I'm all too aware of the way they have rehearsed their movements in the studio using spoken rhythms ('And one-and-two-and-point-and-turn' etc). There's a famous description of the bemused dancers who gave the premiere of Stravinsky's *Rite of Spring*, grimly clinging to their spoken mnemonics while the mayhem of Stravinsky's score raged about them. Even today at dance programmes I often feel I'm hearing one set of rhythms from the dancers' feet pattering on the wooden floor of the stage, and another set emanating from the musicians in the orchestra pit. The dance steps are superimposed on the music, but don't truly arise from it. In some crazy way it makes ballet seem unmusical.

So Mark Morris's choreography meant a lot to me. Everything his dancers did seemed to be suggested by what was going on in the music. After years of irritation at the ballet I suddenly realised that it is possible for a choreographer to be acutely sensitive to music – indeed, to be inspired by it on a moment-to-moment basis, letting the music suggest the precise steps, turns and runs.

Tonight's performance, however, left me perplexed. The lively group dances had Morris's usual wit, but the choreography for Romeo and Juliet themselves was minimal to the point of emptiness. Much of their music is slow and dreamy, and it was as if Morris had decided that if there was no rhythmic activity in the score, there could be no steps for the dancers. Consequently Romeo and Juliet often stood around in thoughtful poses instead of actually dancing. What effect was he aiming at? Was he presenting the dance as a kind of descant to the music, something decorating but not supplanting the main thing itself? Hovering over the production seemed to be some intellectual concept that didn't quite work – such as trying to suggest by lack of movement that Romeo and Juliet were in a non-physical zone, removed from the everyday world into one of spirit. However, there's a difference between sustained slow-moving chords in the orchestra and nearly-immobile dancers on the stage. Long notes played on real instruments vibrate in the air, but a dancer holding a pose doesn't. Around me, the ballet fans in the audience were squirming with frustration.

A first edit of Haydn

The postman brings a CD of my trio playing Haydn piano trios which we recorded in Henry Wood Hall some months ago. This is the dreaded 'first edit' sent by our producer Andrew Keener for our comments and requests. He has already spent a great deal of time putting together what he considers the best selection of takes. Long ago we agreed it was best for him, rather than us, to do this. There are so many factors governing what an individual musician would choose; we're all aware of the danger that whoever has the casting vote would naturally gravitate towards all the takes where they played beautifully themselves, perhaps passing over those where they made a slip, even if someone else had played their best ever version. When several people's agendas are competing, the choice is far from straightforward and not always guided by purely musical principles. Therefore it seems best to let an expert outsider make the selection. Even so, I know from experience that if I question anything I'm not happy with in my own playing, saying I know I played it better than this, Andrew's reply will probably be that there is no other possibility because something unacceptable – a noise, mistake, a note out of tune – rules out every other take. So I know that some of my best playing has been rejected for reasons not to do with me. The same is true of course for all the players.

I make myself sit down and listen to the Haydn. As

always, it comes as a surprise. First of all, the recorded sound quality is not what I remember from our listening during the sessions. Everything seems smaller and boxier, the instruments drier and with less bloom. On my home hi-fi system I can hardly hear the cello line, though I could hear it clearly in the producer's room during the recordings. Secondly, the performance I now hear on disc is not one that we ever gave like that in its entirety. Our producer has chosen the best of this and the best of that, weaving his favourite takes as near as possible into a perfect version. It's therefore a more technically flawless result than we ever achieved in the studio, though that's not to say that we didn't play each section well at some time or other during those three days. The effect of hearing all our most successful playing knitted together is of hearing a more Olympian group than ours, a trio with a daunting level of accuracy and stamina, who never make crude mistakes or let themselves stamp their feet, squeak, scratch a string, cough, swear, make a noise when turning the page, breathe into the microphone, creak the piano stool, or whatever. All these things happen in the recording sessions, but are banned from the disc. Nothing is manipulated, no electronic wizardry is used to clean things up, but our mistakes have been left on the cutting room floor. The final effect is pleasing to one's vanity, but no doubt contributes to the high expectations of audiences everywhere these days, who grow used to the recording, expect our live performance to be equally faultless, and feel let down if it isn't.

Touching pupils

In the news today, we hear that the Musicians' Union has issued guidelines to its members about how to behave towards pupils when teaching them. Teachers are now advised not to touch students when giving music lessons, in order not to run the risk of being accused of 'inappropriate behaviour'. All sorts of musicians are irate about this, including the cellist Julian Lloyd Webber who sensibly made the point that students learn much faster and more surely if you can show them by guiding their hand on the bow, on the timpani stick, or whatever. In response, a spokeman from the MU said that they deal with numerous complaints by children against music teachers, who often conduct their lessons in private, and in a room set aside from the main thoroughfare of the school.

I have also heard some troubling stories about music teachers and their inappropriate behaviour, and there's no doubt that vulnerable students must be protected by sensible guidelines. The trouble is that if you outlaw inappropriate touching, you also outlaw appropriate touching. Yes, all sorts of things can be taught by demonstration, and a teacher can tell a lot just from looking and hearing, but there are many things about playing a musical instrument which are conveyed far more accurately with a gentle guiding hand. In the course of my musical education I had hundreds of lessons with many different teachers, on piano, violin, percussion and chamber music. I encountered lots of touching but never any inappropriate touching; the physical hints were always and only in the context of the music we were discussing. Perhaps I have been lucky, but I imagine my experience was normal. As an occasional teacher myself, I quite often ask a piano student to move aside from the piano stool so that I can sit down and demonstrate something. I usually touch them on the shoulder to attract their attention, and then ask them to move aside. Should I try to stop myself doing this now?

Bob remembers talking to an elderly professor of wind playing who took over from a very popular, handsome young professor whose departure was a matter of sorrow to many of his students. Soon after the new professor began, he was accused of 'inappropriate touching' by two female students. It turned out that they objected to his tapping the correct rhythms on their shoulders as they played. Well, perhaps the tapping of rhythms was annoying, but their response was vindictive, probably motivated by a desire for revenge against their new teacher because he was not as personable as the previous one.

Those who inherit the consequences of teachers standing back from their pupils are the hundreds of physiotherapists who are daily consulted by music students and professional musicians who suffer from all kinds of playing-related aches and pains. One can only imagine that if instrumental teaching were more precise, there would be less need for the ministrations of physiotherapists after things go wrong. Ironically, of course, there is no way of sorting out those physical problems without very specific hands-on treatment. It does seem regrettable and faintly absurd that music teachers all over the country are forbidden from touching their pupils, only to have fairly large numbers of those same pupils heading off to the masseur's couch instead. Are we to return to a Jane Austen-type situation where paid chaperones are to sit in a corner of the room doing embroidery during music lessons?

$\mathcal{E}loquence$

Some friends tell me they went to Cambridge to hear a renowned poet give a lecture. The lecture was, they said, 'probably absolutely brilliant', but unfortunately they could not understand a word of it. People seated around them kept exchanging rueful glances with them. At the end, a vote of thanks was given by someone who managed to praise the poet's speech without referring to anything he had said, presumably because it was too difficult to sum up.

Whenever I hear this kind of thing, I feel that the fault lies with the speaker and not with the audience. My friends, though not academic themselves, are highly intelligent people, interested in many things. Moreover, they were excited about hearing this lecture because they knew that the speaker is considered a wonderful poet. So they were motivated to enjoy his lecture, but in practice it made them feel small. Surely, if you are giving a public speech, it should be possible to express even the most complicated thoughts in ways that a willing listener can follow? Sometimes it seems that there's an inverse relationship between great learning and great communication skills, but I don't see why. Einstein famously said, 'Everything should be as simple as possible, but not simpler.' This leaves open the possibility that there are things not capable of being expressed more simply. But Einstein was probably talking about equations and mathematical formulae. Can there be concepts of literature or poetry so abstruse that they can't be illuminated, even by a master of words who sets out to give a public lecture? I feel sad that when I ask my friends, 'What was the lecture actually about?', I hear their slightly shamefaced answer, 'Well, you know, I'm not absolutely sure.' To me this is not a tribute to the lecturer's towering intellect but rather an indictment of it. How much cleverer to have sent my friends home glowing with the sense that they had understood something really challenging!

$\mathcal{W}$inter journey

John and I meet at English National Opera for our first try-out of Schubert's 'Winterreise' song cycle. Johnny and I were good friends at college, but have gone our separate ways since then, he into opera and I into the very different concert world. As we haven't seen each other for some years, most of my Tube journey into town is unpleasantly taken up with wondering whether I have aged unpalatably in appearance since we last met. This thought didn't used to bother me, but it does now. Our rehearsal space is a little garret room at the top of the building. Mussorgsky's opera *Boris Godunov* has just had its first night, and the room is full of costumes for the chorus, authentically grubby to evoke the feudal Russia of the opera. In between racks of grey worsted jerkins and cloaks there is just room for an upright piano. Against this operatic backdrop our little plainclothes duo feels awfully modest.

We start by talking about the music and the way that singers usually approach it. I was very struck recently by reading the reminiscences of Maria Wagner, a woman who heard Schubert sing, as he used to do at private gatherings if he wanted to demonstrate new songs to his friends. Maria Wagner remarked that she had heard all the great singers of the day, 'but no one sang as Schubert did, and that without a voice'. This is very touching, but also puzzling. What was it about Schubert's singing that seemed superior if he didn't have a good voice?

One thing the story clearly shows is that beauty of tone is not paramount. John has a beautiful voice anyway, but he likes this story and agrees that delivery of the text and its underlying emotion is more important.

We each know the music very well, so we are able to run straight through the songs, pausing to talk about the character of each and the different ways we could do them. John has an interesting approach to the poems, pointing out that less is often more when conveying extreme states. For example he says that when performing the role of someone who's drunk, or is about to have an emotional outburst, it's important to remember that people who are drunk try very hard not to appear so, and people who feel they're about to burst into tears try very hard to hold themselves together. He wants to try this with some of the bleaker, more desperate Schubert songs, hoping to give the impression of a narrator who is forcing himself to keep going, summoning the strength to travel onwards through the winter landscape even though his heart is breaking. We agree there's a fine line between manly restraint and the kind of English understatement we don't want to be accused of. Sometimes less is more, but we mustn't lose sight of the fact that less is usually less.

As John says, the music itself will stop us from erring on the side of emotional coolness. 'You just can't help being taken along by it', he says. 'Once you start to sing, it just grips you. Schubert has composed it in such a way that you can't stand aside from it.' And indeed as we progress through the songs this becomes clear. The music has an extraordinary emotional charge, even when it looks quite sparse on the page. The fact that there are only two of us starts to feel meaningful. John is the only voice, and I am playing the only instrument, so *it all has to be done by us*. He is the wanderer, and I am the landscape full of ice, wind, misleading lights and hostile animals. I soon lose the feeling that we are novices with this music, because it feels obvious what to do, the music providing such a beautiful engine for the words. Or is it the other way round? Whichever it is, the music drives us. I start to have the sense that here under the roof of the building, as we make our way through Schubert's winter journey, the space is becoming charged with an energy that is surely palpable from outside, our little studio somehow glowing in the dark like the room at the top of a lighthouse.

$\mathcal{G}$ut strings

Today I'm in Bath to play the Brahms piano quintet with the Quatuor Mosaïques, an Austrian string quartet specialising in 'period instrument' playing. They play with gut strings on their instruments, as opposed to the steel strings used by most players today. The gut strings have a much softer, shyer, mellower sound with less projecting power – the sound that most classical composers would have known. On the minus side, the tuning is much less stable than with modern strings, leading to an awful lot of tuning in rehearsals and in between movements in the concert. These gut strings are far more sensitive to cold and hot, to damp and dry – which is one reason they were gradually phased out.

Our rehearsal is a nearly comical reversal of the discussions I'm usually involved in about the level of sound projection required. We begin, and play for several minutes before anyone stops to make a comment. During these several pages, I'm struck by how quiet everything is, compared with the beefy and assertive way this piece normally sounds. Eventually, we stop and one of the violinists says, 'Up until now, we've only been playing loudly. Can we please remember that many of the passages are marked quiet?' And from then on, most of the requests directed at me are to ask me to play more softly. I can hardly believe my ears; usually I'm exhorted to play louder. Our whole rehearsal seems to be an exploration of how many different shades of quiet we can discover. It's actually a refreshing experience and makes it easy to bring out the intimate qualities of the piece, often lost in the competitive 'I can make a louder sound than you can' atmosphere of many modern performances. It also makes it easier to bring out all the delicate nuances which Brahms marks in the score. All the same, despite the many advantages of playing with gut strings, the unfamiliarly quiet sound level in our concert makes me feel as if I have jumped into a bath, expecting it to be very hot, only to find myself in tepid water.

It makes me realise what a vicious spiral we have been locked into: halls have become bigger and bigger, so instruments have to be made more powerful to reach to the back of the hall. These louder instruments are physically tougher to play, so more strength is required, and more musicians start to suffer from aches and strains. The volume produced by modern instruments has damaged some players' hearing. Today we've reached the absurd situation where orchestral players have to be protected from one another's sound by Perspex screens separating the brass from the strings and so on.

In the concert with the Mosaïques I'm very struck by what these Austrian musicians talk about in the interval: the relative merits of different quartets by Mendelssohn, which quartets are more satisfying, which show him at his best, which ones point the way to what he could have achieved in the future had he lived longer. After the concert, the conversation continues animatedly over supper. We discuss Brahms and the kind of sound he would have hoped to hear, the link between his chamber music and his symphonies, the difference between him and Mendelssohn, the late blossoming of one and the early blossoming of the other. We even talk a bit about our performance.

This is very different to the conversations which British musicians generally have during or after concerts. In no way are British players less talented or less committed, but with us it's almost a point of pride not to talk about the music. Most Brits are desperate not to be thought pretentious. We love our music, but prefer whatever absorbing emotions were involved in the performance to be left on the platform, not in danger of being sullied by small talk; afterwards, by tacit agreement, we talk of other things. But for my Austrian colleagues, music is a topic which spills naturally over from the concert to the dressing-room and to the café afterwards. I find this so striking that I ask them whether classical music still feels important in Austria? Looking slightly puzzled at the question, they say it does. Hasn't it been pushed to the edge of cultural activities by pop music and so on? No, they say, still looking slightly puzzled. 'You don't feel that people consider classical music stuffy?' 'No.' 'Do you feel that being a classical musician has some status attached to it?' 'Oh yes, definitely. Austrians are proud of their classical music heritage.' 'Would you say that the parents of your children's friends are impressed if you turn up at the school gates carrying a violin case?' 'Oh yes, I think so, yes.'

It reminds me of Bruno Schrecker, ex-cellist of the Allegri Quartet, talking about a childhood in Vienna, about how when a member of the Vienna Philharmonic got on the bus carrying a musical instrument, people would stand up to offer him their seat. This story has always made me feel wistful and sad.

December …

Joining up the dots

A friend of mine is playing in the orchestra for *Phantom of the Opera* at the moment. This long-running musical by Andrew Lloyd Webber is so successful that the members of the orchestra are actually salaried, but they have a certain amount of leeway for taking time off and appointing 'deputies', and this is how my friend came to be there. From where she sits in the orchestra pit, she can glance up and see the faces in the front row of the stalls, gilded by the stage lighting. Every night, at the end of the performance, many of those illuminated faces are streaked with tears.

Although it's easy to understand that the emotional resolution of a dramatic plot can move people to tears in the theatre, I often have the same experience in the concert hall. The lighting over the audience is usually too dim to make out many faces, but I can see the first few rows clearly enough, and the best of our pieces often make people cry. Though our music is 'abstract', wordless and rarely has an explicit narrative, listeners clearly experience the same kind of 'storytelling' catharsis that they do at an opera. As they listen to our instrumental music, they enter into the sense of 'a journey' and are led by the music through the same kind of dramas, conflicts and resolutions that are laid out more plainly in the theatre. I often feel that the composers urgently need to express things in narrative form, and that listeners are hungry to receive it.

My daughter Maya did some work experience at People's Archive, a project which invites eminent scientists to talk at length about their work and their lives. The participants devote several days of relaxed filming to mulling over how it all happened, how the episodes of their life ran into their work and vice versa. They're deliberately given lots of time to make connections between things, to understand how one idea led to another – in other words, to capture 'the whole narrative'. I asked Vitek Tracz, whose idea the Archive was, whether anyone had ever said that there was no narrative, that their life or work has just been a collection of random incidents. 'Never. Everyone's convinced there has been a storyline. They all think that everything adds up. It all makes sense to them in retrospect, even if not at the time'.

Brain cells

While doing the ironing, I'm idly listening to Melvyn Bragg on the radio. A group of scientists are discussing the fact that when you try to hear music in your imagination, the brain cells which are active in this endeavour are the same brain cells which are active when you're actually listening to music played externally. The same for visual imagining: if you're told to visualise a square, for example, the same brain cells are used as when actually looking at a square.

This fascinates me because it implies that practising a musical instrument in one's head could be a very valid form of practice. 'Think nine times and play once', was a wise remark I heard in György Sebök's piano masterclasses, though he brought it up to remind us that for most musicians the balance is exactly the other way round. They play nine times and think once. But practising in one's head is certainly something that teachers could recommend to their students now that there is so much repetitive strain injury in the world of performing musicians. If the same brain cells are involved, then presumably one could do some genuinely good work without going near the instrument – at least in the field of interpretation, memorising, going over patterns of fingering and so on.

I have known a few musicians – mainly historians and musicologists – who could get as much pleasure from reading a score and imagining the sound in their heads as they did from attending a real performance. My old Cambridge tutor Philip Radcliffe, for instance; he could certainly imagine music vividly enough to be satisfied by a purely mental performance. Indeed, we students used to feel frustrated with him sometimes if we persuaded him to come to a live concert, because he didn't particularly seem to notice what had actually happened in their performance, hearing it mainly as confirmation of the score he already had in his head. He'd come round afterwards and say, 'What a marvellous piece that is!' but would never comment on how we had played it. I don't think this was because we'd done a bad job; it was more that Philip mapped any live performance onto the model he had already internalised.

There is a difference, of course, between imagined music and live music, and it is to do with the way the live sound impacts on the rest of your body, the nervous system in particular. Watching the players is important, too; the combination of aural and visual components can be very powerful. I'm fairly good at hearing music in my head, but I don't think an imaginary rendering has ever actually moved me to tears, or made my heart beat faster, in the way that a live performance can. Nor do I think that imagining a piece of music, even recollecting a superb performance, can give me shivers down the spine as sometimes happens in a live concert (and occasionally happens to me even when I am the performer). I suppose the same brain cells are involved in both imagining and actually hearing, but the brain is not the only part of the body which responds to music.

Someone else's voice

A phone call this morning from Sweden, from the head of the team organising a 'Dialogue Seminar' about my writings next month in Stockholm. They're planning a concert at which I'll play, and extracts from my books will be read. They've had the idea of getting someone else, not me, to read the excerpts from my books. Now they call to say they're excited by the fact that the well-known actress Gunnel Lindblom has agreed to read the excerpts at the concert. Gunnel Lindblom is famous for her appearances in Ingmar Bergman's enigmatic films. A blonde, grave beauty now in her seventies, she is sure to give my words an extra authority.

This will be a new experience for me. On the rare occasions that my words have been read out, I have been the one doing the reading. What will it be like to hear someone else speaking my lines? None of my lines were written in the knowledge that someone would read them out loud. Famously, writers are not particularly good at reading out their own work, and audiences often complain that when they hear the author speak, they fail to hear the voice which they imagined and sometimes 'heard' quite strongly during their silent reading. The playwright Mark Ravenhill recently remarked wisely that a writer's 'voice' is not the same thing as the sound that comes out of the writer's mouth. Audiences are deceived if they think that a writer is the ideal reader of his or her work;

more to the point, they are wrong if they think that the writer will sound as they believe he or she *should* sound.

Words read silently to oneself and words read aloud are travelling on two different tracks, and possibly to two different destinations. Sometimes it's wonderful to hear an author's work read out loud by someone who knows how to do it, or who has a beautiful voice. A couple of years ago I remember Seamus Heaney on hearing T.S. Eliot's *Four Quartets* read out by actor Robert Speaight: 'It was a crucial moment of illumination. What was hypnotic read aloud had been perplexing when sight-read for meaning only.' I try to imagine myself sitting in the theatre in Stockholm listening to Gunnel Lindblom taking over my voice. Will she reveal shades of meaning I hadn't imagined? Will it be a kind of out-of-body experience for me? If she reads the excerpts in Swedish, I won't know whether she is getting the sense right or not. If she reads in English, I think I will feel, like Bottom, translated!

Inverse snobbery

This week the office of the Mayor of London, Boris Johnson, made my heart lift with an unexpected statement. 'Too often, it is presumed that young people will only like art they can immediately relate to. ...Working-class students may be steered towards popular culture like hip-hop, new media and film on the basis that they will find older art forms such as opera or ballet irrelevant. This is extremely patronising.'

'There's been a kind of inverse snobbery about culture', said his culture chief Munira Mirza. 'I've seen the minutes of meetings. There's been a slight sniffiness about culture, that it had to have a wider value, and you always had to justify it.'

Reading this report came as a great relief. I have no argument with hip-hop, new media or film – they have reinvigorated other art forms and bring pleasure to huge numbers of people. My problem has been with the deliberate sidelining of other, particularly older forms of culture such as classical music. Yes, indeed, for a long time now we have had to justify it, prove that it has 'a wider value', and even explain why we thought it should survive. This has had a lowering effect on morale over a long period. We are veterans of applications to grant-making bodies for small amounts of funding to run our own projects. The forms are always extremely long and detailed, sometimes requiring us to hire a professional who understands how to supply the information in the jargon-laden way that some councils want to see it.

We'd love people to come and hear us play, but it is dispiriting when we're sent to proselytise amongst people who don't care if they hear us or not. Outreach projects, a splendid idea in themselves, have become so important that they have threatened to overtake and eclipse the core projects. Everyone in the British music world knows it's often easier to get funding for an outreach workshop than for the actual concert which inspired it. This would be justified if outreach were grabbing lots of young people and turning them into concert-goers, but it is very hard to make the right impact on the wrong territory, particularly if that territory is a noisy school hall with bells ringing and pupils ducking in and out of the audience to attend other clubs and commitments. I've done my share of outreach work over the years. Occasionally you get an encouraging response from an individual, as long as they can find a way to speak to you unseen by their friends. But the kind of music we play has no instant cachet for today's youngsters. I've never forgotten my dismay when a headmaster said to me, after a schools concert, 'I think it's very good for our pupils to see that there are people like you who actually choose to spend their lives engaged in something very unfashionable and eccentric.' He meant it kindly, but it didn't feel good.

The kind of music we play needs a different sort of presentation. It belongs to the Slow Food tradition of cultural dishes lovingly built, long stirred and relished by people with the time and appetite to appreciate them. And to continue the food analogy, you can't just march into some classroom with a pot of classic Bolognese sauce and expect a group of stressed youngsters to intuit the whole atmosphere, aroma and sound of a traditional Italian trattoria, let alone to understand Italian.

Northern lights

Watched a delightful programme about the actress Joanna Lumley's journey to the Arctic Circle in the hope of seeing the Northern Lights, which she had longed to experience since she saw an illustration of them in a storybook when she was seven years old. In the course of the trip, she visited the Sami people and went on a journey with a reindeer herdsman. When darkness fell, they sat in his tent with a well-known Sami singer of traditional songs known as 'yoiks'. Yoiks, it seems, are not exactly songs as we know them, but spontaneous celebrations of people and places, or indeed spontaneous expressions of dilemmas and situations, their new words fitted to old 'yoik' phrases. Yoiks can be made up to capture the essence of a person, and sung to remind oneself of that person, or even to convey an impression of them to another person. By way of demonstration, the conversation in the tent was interrupted when the Sami singer suddenly broke off to close his eyes, throw his head back and sing a few lines about his host, the reindeer herder, who looked on solemnly and proudly. The singer's voice rose high in the air, fluttered down again, and he resumed talking. It seemed a wonderful way to give voice to those moments when one feels the need for something heightened, but hesitates to try and put one's feeling into ordinary words.

Joanna Lumley asked whether there would be an appropriate

yoik she could learn so that she could salute the Northern Lights with it, should she be lucky enough to see them. But the Sami singer frowned at this and shook his head. He explained that there is no yoik for the Northern Lights. 'No, no. You must not address them. And you must not tease them.' The same sentiment had been expressed by an apparently down-to-earth physicist at the Arctic Circle observatory where they study the Northern Lights: 'If you see them, do not wave at them.' How lovely that the Sami people have no yoik for one of the world's most spectacular natural phenomena, one that takes place above the roofs of their homes and must seem to belong to them. 'Whereof you cannot speak, thereof you must be silent.'

*P*reparing to make a recording

My trio is about to make a record which I've been rather dreading because I know it's going to be physically very demanding. We've chosen three Czech pieces by Smetana, Martinů and the contemporary composer Petr Eben. All are virtuosic, particularly the Smetana which is highly emotional as well as grand and theatrical, with a flamboyant piano part. The three pieces amount to about 75 minutes of music, about the maximum for a CD, and we have three days to make the disc. This may sound fairly liberal, but from past experience I know we never manage to record more than 25–30 minutes of music in a full day's work, generally spilling over into the evening. We'll play each movement over and over again, and then we'll progress to playing sections of each movement over and over, and finally we'll focus in on particularly tricky small sections which will be played many times as well, until they are as perfect as we can make them. It's a little like the process of watching fractals being created on a computer display, going deeper and deeper into the heart of patterns.

In the recording sessions we'll play for many more hours than we normally do each day, at full intensity and full volume. This is something for which it seems impossible to prepare, as you can only prepare by doing it, and the actuality always comes as a shock. I have started to lie awake at night worrying about it, which is totally counter-productive as it makes it less likely that I will be mentally up to the task when the recording sessions actually begin. I lie awake practising all the tricky bits in my head, playing them slowly, playing them fast, and by way of interlude, breaking off to antici- pate the kind of situations which always arise in recording sessions, where we get cross with one another and spend half our time privately debating whether it is the moment to say so or not. It's Sod's Law that when any one of us succeeds in playing something exactly as we imagine it, someone else will choose that moment to cough or scrape their chair, and the lovely moment will join the 'can't be used' list compiled by our producer. Even if someone is suddenly visited by the angel of inspiration and plays divinely for a whole take, there will be plenty of other reasons why the take will have to be jettisoned: planes passing overhead, trains rumbling below, rubbish lorries in the street outside.

We always believe we're sincerely free of mannerisms and passing fancies. We aim at a timeless result which has indisput- able musical value, and which we hope will speak to people at other times and in other places. But these days I'm often haunted by something that Bob pointed out to me when discussing some of his favourite recordings of the past: that no performer can escape from the tastes of their own time. Until this was pointed out, I think I was labouring under the delu- sion that players of previous eras may have had their quaint little foibles, but that we didn't.

No matter how timeless you think your interpretation is (and maybe it is), you can't help being a living example of your own particular era's views on sound production, histor- ical correctness, attitudes to strictness or flexibility, approach to tempo, and so on. Even if you think you have succeeded in transcending the contemporary views on these matters, there will inevitably come a time when other people will listen to your recording with a smile and say, 'Listen to that! Isn't that so typical of the early twenty-first century!' What it is that will strike them as 'typical of it' I have no way of knowing. When I go into the producer's backstage studio to listen to what we've done, I sometimes catch myself trying to throw my mind into the future and 'listen back' to our playing for signs of mere temporality. It can't be done, of course. You can hear slips of intention and of execution, but you can't guess what will strike a future listener as funny or quaint. And certainly you can't know what may strike them as precious and delightful, an example of something that has been lost.

French Impressionist

I'm practising four of the pieces from Ravel's *Miroirs* for the concert in Stockholm next week. I've loved these piano pieces since an astute teacher put them in front of me when I was a first-year college student. They're a musical equivalent of French Impressionist painting, vivid little nature scenes involving sad birds, a boat on the sea, night moths, a valley full of bells. It's a curious thing that both Ravel and Debussy, who loved to paint little scenes in music and to give them descriptive titles, very rarely put any people into those scenes. In that sense their music has the same feeling as, say, Monet's paintings of flowers, bridges and water. Human beings and their emotions have been purposely subtracted from the stage, leaving nature to exult in its own aliveness. Ravel's *Miroirs* succeed in giving the impression that no human hands were involved in their making, and that no human presence runs through the scenes. The sad birds call in a forest with no one to hear them. The bells ring out over a valley empty of visitors. The night moths come out when everyone is asleep. Even the boat depicted in 'Une barque sur l'ocean' seems to be tossed this way and that by the waves, with no sailor to steer a different course.

To play music by a composer really attuned to the possibilities of the piano is always a distinctive feeling. There's a lot of very fine music written for the piano, of course, but not all of it lies well under the hands or is a pleasure to play. Even Beethoven and Bach, 'without whom, not' (as Bob would say) often go their musical way without regard for the feeling of the hands on the keyboard, for the dance of the bones and muscles of the fingers. But composers like Chopin, Ravel, Rachmaninov, Debussy, whose piano music is often terribly difficult to play, seem nevertheless to be composing 'with the grain' of the keyboard, and with an instinctive understanding of the shapes that fingers and hands can make without distortion. Their piano music seems to move in a different and more compassionate spatial geometry. It's hugely intricate to work out how to move around the keyboard in the way they demand, often with astonishingly complex layers and patterns involving lightning fast reflexes and a laser-like control of touch and tone. It takes ages to figure it out, often requiring a very long period of building up from slow practice until you've mastered the necessary speeds.

Even then, it often remains somehow on the cusp of what's possible. For example, I learned the Ravel piano trio years ago, but it doesn't get easier: in performance it still feels as though he had planned for it to march on the very edge of physical achievability. This kind of well-written, demanding but idiomatic piano music gives a feeling of particular pleasure and satisfaction once you've 'cracked it'. As a pianist you feel that you are fully occupied, but occupied with something that repays your effort and is sympathetic to your physical construction. My private accolade for such music is when the experience of playing it rings true with the wonderful phrase that Nathaniel Hawthorne used to describe his happy marriage with his wife Sophie: 'there is no vacancy in my mind any more than in my heart'.

In the studio

I'm back from the first of three days in Henry Wood Hall making the trio's new record. I get so keyed up for recordings that I'm very brittle, anxious about my stamina, worried about my hands getting tired and stiff, conscious that every note is going to be scrutinised by experts with the score and a red pencil in front of them. Our producer will not let go if he knows there are any obvious mistakes or missing notes on the recording – and of course accuracy is only the beginning of what we hope to achieve. I'm so focused on the task in hand, and so unwilling to be diverted from it that I feel like slapping anyone who dares to ask me anything trivial, such as how my Christmas shopping is going. I find it painful to hear members of the recording team chatting about other matters. Even though I realise that this is the umpteenth disc they've collaborated on this year, I feel quite undermined by the evidence that this may not be as momentous an occasion for them as it is for us. I'm very close to asking them please not to talk in front of me about restaurant bookings, holiday plans, or other artists' recording sessions which are coming up, especially if the prospect seems to amuse them. Somehow the thought that they'll all be here again next week, recording something else, perhaps reminiscing about that bad-tempered pianist they worked with last week, makes me feel small and unimportant at just the time when I want to feel that all our energies are crystallising around something special. I realise it's perverse of me to feel this way when I dislike recording.

Recording is a very strange thing. There's no audience, so it's very hard to work up any sense of performance energy, and yet there looms over us the awareness of a potential audience of individuals listening one day to our recording on their home hi-fi, computer or iPod. The empty hall feels somehow populated by thousands of ghostly future listeners, who in my imagination float somewhere near the very high ceiling of our recording venue, Henry Wood Hall, gazing down on us inscrutably. Our performance will remain fixed once it's committed to disc, so we have to be able to live with it. That means that we have to pursue two tracks simultaneously, one focused on accuracy and one on expression and meaning. We each know that our own mistakes could ruin the 'take' for the others, and this knowledge seems to bring down a bell jar over each person's head, isolating us from one another at a time when we should be closely co-operating. It is very much the opposite of fun.

Although we're all concentrating fiercely, I find that as each take ends I immediately lose the sensation of how it went, and in particular my sense of how it compares to any of the other takes. It feels impossible both to play and to retain enough distance to be analytic. We rely on our producer Andrew Keener to tell us whether that was the best version we've yet played, or whether there are still targets to reach. He knows us well enough now to say candidly when he feels we could do better – and also to reassure us when we can relax safe in the knowledge that it has been well captured. He takes care to phrase any criticisms with delicate tact, for which I'm grateful, because I get so overwrought that anything more direct would undoubtedly make me snap. At the end of a day like this I feel a peculiar sense of depletion, as though someone has reached inside me with an invisible spoon and scooped out some of my marrow. I actually feel as if I've lost some essential nutrients, and am good for nothing more than staring zombie-like into space for the rest of the evening. Oddly, this weariness will be absent from the disc, which after skilful editing will come out sounding freshly-scrubbed and zestful.

$\mathcal{M}$agnetic repulsion

There are bad days as well as good days in chamber music. When it's going well, being with one's colleagues is the nicest of things. When it's going badly, it feels like the first circle of hell, where (according to Dante) non-Christian thinkers and creative artists live, unable to enter heaven, but enjoying a little freedom in the heart of hell. I suppose it is because when people make themselves vulnerable to one another, they run big risks.

The problem is not the music, but what happens when it stops. Outsiders might think that if certain people share an appreciation of music, an instrumental technique, an ability to express themselves, a sense of structure or rhythm or intonation, they would be compatible across the board, but – maddeningly – it's not nearly so simple. There can be a strange separation between the rapport that exists between musical partners and the distance that opens up between them the minute they stop playing. It sometimes seems almost as if the more intense one's musical communication, the more one seeks refuge from it by shutting down channels of communication when the music stops. Sometimes this feeling goes even further and passes beyond the neutral zone into a kind of rejection, like a horse refusing a fence.

Novelists, even those admired for their writing about music and musicians, usually seem to imagine that musicians live in a continual frisson of rapport which spills over from their performances into the rest of their lives. They fall joyfully from the concert platform into late-night confidences and more. These situations do occur, but in my experience mostly between people who don't know one another all that well. I believe it is more often the case that people who work together over a long period, and are intensely involved in their shared musical responsibilities, are actually desperate to go back into their shells afterwards. Rapport during the performance can be very real, but it does not always bleed into other areas of life.

The tension between people who are musically compatible is one of the lesser-known paradoxes about life in an ensemble. Music is often described as a metaphor for life, but it's sometimes a metaphor that remains in an ideal world. I'm well aware that it's not just me who feels this sense of alienation outside music; both from observation and from hearing other musicians' anecdotes over many years, I've realised it's a widespread phenomenon. Sometimes it feels as if as soon as the music stops, the members of a group become like magnets with their like poles together, agitating to repel one another.

$\mathcal{I}_n$ Vienna with no hat

On my afternoon off between trio rehearsal and concert in Vienna, I walk into the city centre to have a look round the cathedral. Though half of me simply wants to rest, the other half doesn't want to be the kind of loser who goes all the way to Vienna and only sees the inside of a hotel room. Snow falls on the big fur hats and coats of the Viennese shoppers, and I feel very un-Austrian walking beside them with my bare head.

Whenever I travel professionally, the sight of bustling local life strikes me rather differently to how it strikes me when I'm a tourist. When I'm on holiday I like to sink in to the local atmosphere and pretend to be one of them. As a performer, however, I can't help feeling slightly intimidated by how effortlessly the life of the city seems to be proceeding without my help. Can they really need a concert by me? Do they even know about it? I find myself gazing at people in the street and wondering whether any of them will be in tonight's audience. My eye falls on a long series of 'stars', plaques set into the pavement in the main shopping street to commemorate famous musicians from Mozart and Haydn to Yehudi Menuhin and Claudio Abbado. This is cheering evidence of the status of classical musicians in Vienna.

And indeed, our audience that evening seems to me to be perched bright-eyed on the edge of their seats, gazing up at us with alacrity. This is striking because I sometimes have the feeling that audiences don't really regard us as live human beings, rather as a spectacle to be passively viewed as if they were watching television. The Viennese concert-goers, by contrast, look positively agog. 'Go on, tell us!' they seem to say, and it inspires me to play my best. The audience cheers and cheers at the end, apparently not wanting to let us go even after lots of curtain calls and two encores. Many individual members of the audience seem to be trying to catch my eye to indicate to me with smiles and nods how much they enjoyed the evening. Afterwards, when I go into the next door restaurant for a drink, I'm applauded by the assembled diners as I walk to my table at the far end of the room. This does not tend to happen in London.

Late that evening, my daughter Maya, responding to my happy e-mail report of the occasion, comes up with the brilliant suggestion that I appoint the Viennese as my 'audience in residence'. They would all have to come to my house as required and sit in my living-room, beaming. 'It would be like an artist-in-residence position, but without all the extra travel for you', she says shrewdly.

The nest

From my desk, and also when I'm propped up in bed with a book, I look out over the roofs opposite to an enormously tall lone tree in the park beyond. Twenty years ago when my daughter was small, some birds came and built a nest near the very top of the tree. When I was feeding my daughter, I often used to look out at the birds feeding their young and feel a sense of camaraderie. The spindly branches swayed alarmingly in the wind, sometimes bending so far to one side or another that I was afraid the contents of the nest would be tipped out and the baby birds would fall before they had had a chance to learn how to fly. The parent birds sometimes had to approach the nest at a sharp angle because of the swaying branches. It struck me as an extreme location for a nest, certainly out of reach of predators, but so high and precarious that it must actually have caused more problems than it solved. Somehow I developed an emotional need to see those birds succeed with their crazy choice of home. As the years went by, I was surprised to see that the nest remained lodged in the topmost branches, and in some years it was used by other birds with frontier spirit. I could only see it clearly in autumn and winter, when the leaves disappeared and the nest was once again outlined blackly against the sky, defying the storms, still clinging to its perch.

'*Spinning*'

It's wonderful to be in Stockholm for my Dialogue Seminar, several sessions and a concert organised by the Royal Technical University at which my writings are discussed by different groups of Swedish researchers from various fields: maths, philosophy, engineering, medicine, teaching, computing, religion and music. They've agreed to read certain of my texts beforehand and to prepare their own written or spoken responses, which are shared with the rest of us during the seminar. This multi-faceted focus on my written work has never happened to me before, and to say that I'm elated by the prospect is an understatement. I had imagined our discussions taking place against a snowy backdrop, but the weather is grey and rainy like it is in London. It doesn't matter, so great is my pleasure at being involved in what feels like the kind of academy that used to convene in the olive groves of ancient Greece, all sorts of people bringing their own tales and questions. Delivered quietly in English, but with melodious Swedish intonation, the contributions of my Stockholm colleagues feel particularly thoughtful.

My final seminar is with a group of Swedish doctors who have been discussing the links between the communication problems which musicians encounter as they work with other musicians, and the problems which face doctors as they explore the best way to collaborate with patients. One of them comments that his consultations often feel like improvised jazz, following an underlying structure (of medical knowledge) but creating a unique response from the ingredients which present themselves at that moment, never to be repeated exactly. We discuss notation, and how musicians find that there's often an inverse relationship between the amount of instructions given in the musical score and the ease of interpreting the music. Edward Elgar commented that the more helpful and precise instructions he tried to give, the more it seemed to confuse musicians. He compared his own scores to those of Mozart, who wrote very little in addition to the notes, but whose meaning seems perfectly clear. Our chairman Bo Goranzon reminds us of a wise remark by Diderot who said, 'If you want to be understood, don't go into detail.' The doctors say that it's obvious a musician won't be a better musician if he or she is given more instructions to follow. By contrast, though, they say doctors are given more and more instructions to follow, and more rules to observe. These are designed to make them better doctors, but often the result is that after following various protocols, there's very little time left for the sort of old-fashioned diagnostic skill which consists in letting the patient talk until they start to reveal, whether intentionally or not and whether in words or body language, what they *really* want to talk about. We discuss the skill of observation and how, if you have the time to develop it, extra rules and instructions become irrelevant. Being observant is a crucial skill in both our fields, medicine and performing music, and we talk about whether it can be learned or has to be innate.

At the end I ask the doctors whether they think that singing or playing music can have a beneficial effect on the body. They say yes, certainly; doing something you like can lower your stress hormones and your heart rate. But that could happen with any pleasant hobby, and I mean more than that: I wonder if music itself has an impact on one's body, if the soundwaves and the vibrations act as a physical tonic, especially if one's immersed in them over many years. Could one become marinaded in music? Could one slowly become cured, like a piece of leather? The word 'cured' hangs in the air between us.

There's a longish diplomatic-sounding pause while they consider their answer, then one of them suddenly smiles and says, 'I've heard that when cats spin, they actually heal themselves through the vibrations.' When cats spin? It's my turn to smile. 'You mean when cats purr?' 'Is that what you call it in English? Yes, the noise they make when they're happy. The purring helps them to become well. Cats don't have as much illness as dogs, and they recover faster. Maybe the healthful vibration they make is like what happens to you when you sing or play, is that what you mean?' Now everyone starts to smile at the thought that music could be a human equivalent of purring.

$$\mathcal{H}eavenly \ voices$$

To Cambridge on a winter day to hear a service in the Chapel of King's College. The great building is in darkness apart from candles burning in the choir stalls and at various points around the walls. Above us, the intricately vaulted ceiling hovers like golden lacework. Shortly before the entrance of the choir, the organ music stops and the whole audience falls silent for what feels like several minutes. This peaceful, unanimous silence is the most therapeutic thing I've experienced for a while.

A medieval building is an ideal place in which to hear the choral music of Palestrina, Byrd, Orlando Gibbons and Bach. On such occasions this ancient music always seems so much more haunting and appropriate than anything written in the centuries since. The choir advances in procession from the back of the Chapel, pausing at various points to stand and sing a motet or anthem. Before they pass through the organ screen and vanish into the choir stalls, they turn and sing to those of us in the Antechapel. Candlelit in their red cassocks and white surplices, they seem timeless, a scene repeated for hundreds of years now. Their mouths open in the O which I sometimes picture during the Latin carol *In dulci jubilo*: 'Alpha es et O'.

Once again I'm struck by the mystery of music. Although I'm a musician myself and know what it's like to perform to an audience, it still seems profoundly mysterious when I'm in the audience witnessing someone else making music. I feel almost shy and deferential as I watch the choir, as though their skill is something 'other', something of which I have no experience. It's simultaneously clear that without their particular voices and talent, these harmonies wouldn't be called into being and made to resonate soothingly around us, and yet it also seems that the music immediately lifts clear of the musicians and 'turns in the evening air', as if it has merely used them as a brief stepping-stone on its way to the mystical realm where it belongs. Undoubtedly the singers are totally responsible for the beautiful effect they create, yet the music seems magically independent of them, as though they just happen to be the people who have opened the gates this evening and set it free. Scientists tell us that they still don't really know what music is 'for' in evolutionary terms. As I sit there in the dark, it's good to be reminded that music is a gift, even for the giver.